How Seniors Are Saving the World

For Bobbie Harris —
Years of Friendship,
Hilarity, Love —
Thelma

How Seniors Are Saving the World

Retirement Activism to the Rescue!

Thelma Reese
and BJ Kittredge

ROWMAN & LITTLEFIELD
Lanham • Boulder • New York • London

Published by Rowman & Littlefield
An imprint of The Rowman & Littlefield Publishing Group, Inc.
4501 Forbes Boulevard, Suite 200, Lanham, Maryland 20706
www.rowman.com

6 Tinworth Street, London SE11 5AL, United Kingdom

British Library Cataloguing in Publication Information Available

Library of Congress Cataloging-in-Publication Data

Names: Reese, Thelma, 1933– author. | Kittredge, BJ, 1944– author.
Title: How seniors are saving the world : retirement activism to the rescue! / Thelma Reese and BJ Kittredge.
Description: Lanham : Rowman & Littlefield Publishers, [2020] | Includes bibliographical references and index. | Summary: "Retirement does not mean retirement from life. It can be a time of fulfillment, activism, and contribution. The men and women profiled in this book are focused outward, repairing problems and contributing to others through their communities, their connections, and the world around them" — Provided by publisher.
Identifiers: LCCN 2019051026 (print) | LCCN 2019051027 (ebook) | ISBN 9781538126974 (cloth ; alk. paper) | ISBN 9781538126981 (epub)
Subjects: LCSH: Retirees—Political activity. | Older people—Political activity. | Social action.
Classification: LCC HQ1061 .R375 2020 (print) | LCC HQ1061 (ebook) | DDC 320.086/96—dc23
LC record available at https://lccn.loc.gov/2019051026
LC ebook record available at https://lccn.loc.gov/2019051027

♾™ The paper used in this publication meets the minimum requirements of American National Standard for Information Sciences—Permanence of Paper for Printed Library Materials, ANSI/NISO Z39.48-1992.

This book is dedicated to the people who are depicted within its pages and to the countless others whose selfless devotion to causes beyond themselves heal the wounds of the world and improve all of our lives. They are the people who embody Vaclav Havel's words:

> It is I who must begin. . . . Once I begin—once I try—here and now, right where I am, not excusing myself by saying that things would be easier elsewhere, without grand speeches and ostentatious gestures, but all the more persistently—to live in harmony with the "voice of Being," as I understand it within myself—as soon as I begin that, I suddenly discover, to my surprise, that I am neither the only one, nor the first, nor the most important one to have set out upon that road. . . . Whether all is really lost or not depends entirely upon whether or not I am lost.

Contents

A Conversation
between the Authors

$\mathcal{D}$ear Reader,

In case you'd like to get to know us before you start reading, we got together for a sidewalk brunch recently and recorded our thoughts about what we planned, hoped for, and some of the things we found writing this book. We edited the recording to remove repetitions and interruptions by the waitstaff, but what you read is our verbatim conversation and a reflection of how we were able to work together so harmoniously. Thelma's speech is in regular type, and BJ's is in italics.

Best wishes,
BJ and Thelma

⟞➤●⟝

So, we're talking about what this book is going to be, and why we are doing it.

And what we hope might come of it.

Most of the rationale for the book can be found in the introduction. But really, we have had to figure out not only why we're doing it, but how—what the book will look like, what will make it inviting and easy for the reader to access.

And to get the most important part of the message.

Exactly. Of course, each reader will be bringing a lot to the experience of reading this book, and many of the readers will be activists themselves. In fact, had we had the opportunity to know them, they would be in it.

Definitely.

So what do we think is important for the reader to get?

I think that besides the specific activism, the reader sees the value of being proactive. I find it so interesting to see how these people share their development. For each of them, it's like a winding river, and they didn't know what was around the next bend, but they were prepared for that place. Sometimes people are reluctant to think about doing something they haven't done before because they don't know where to go to start. Sometimes they think, "Oh, I didn't even think about this before I was sixty!" But what you can *do, as some of these people have, is come with fresh eyes and fresh experience and wisdom.*

Yes. You don't realize how much you are bringing with you, and so it can be a time of self-discovery, where you realize that you have something to give you didn't even know you had.

Exactly.

While you are saving the world or saving someone else, you're saving yourself or discovering yourself.

That's always the way, I think, when you step out of yourself without taking stock of what you are going to gain from this.

I also know that I find, as I always do, something special in learning somebody else's story. Somehow it's a human thing to want to hear a story, know a story, tell a story, and I think I will find it so satisfying to learn more stories.

I also think that we are living through a tumultuous time in our society, and what we have here is action-oriented, positive, and self-fulfilling, and that's a good thing to have. I'm for any of those "not bad things to have" when there is so much that is negative around us.

Yes, it gives us balance. Knowing about positive activism, the kind that's aimed at fixing the world, also provides a focus that can take the reader, as well as the authors, away from some of the difficulties we experience, not just having to do with the turmoil in the world, but the changes in ourselves we may find difficult to deal with.

I used to wonder if I retired, "What would I do with all of my time?" And I found that there are too many things and not enough time, but this work is different for me. It's multi-layered. It feels like putting bricks in the wall of something solid that we're building from the foundation up.

It's a real learning experience. For me, it's a time that validates the idea that we keep developing, that we're not creatures who reach a certain stage and just stop. If we're lucky enough to still be able to think and express ideas, then we can still grow, contribute, be of use, be of value, count.

And it takes us out of our comfort zones and into pieces of the world that we would not have been exposed to otherwise. One of the upsides is being reminded that people can be so good, and there can be so much goodness without the need for payback, for compensation.

And the people are all so different.

It's really amazing to me how different each person's story is in almost every way. Just as our readers are.

That's one of the key things that I have learned interviewing people over the years, particularly with this topic of what one is actually willing to do and not just talk about. Of course, the talking about a cause *is* the doing in some cases, where you are persuading people about a cause. I find the idea of devoting one's actual actions and abilities to something beyond yourself very inspiring.

The example is often what gathers people to a cause. People are attracted naturally to success, and once you start with an idea and *a plan, even limited success can attract others.*

True. And that's why some people who don't start out that way become leaders when they are devoted to a cause. But for most, that has nothing to do with why they start and may never have anything to do with it. Fixing something is what they have in mind, and as they continue doing what seems like mundane tasks, it's the cause that matters, not the position, the title, or the recognition. I think it's important that each person we interview be given his or her own place in the book as a chapter with a "How to Connect!" section at the end in case the reader is inspired to look further into what that person is working on.

Yes, the reader may find things in the activist's toolbox (or sewing kit) that they never thought of doing. The readers are as different, as individuals, as the people we interview. With "How to Connect!" the reader would be able to contact either that person or an organization that person is involved in. It might send them to the internet to learn even more about the cause.

All of this brings up thoughts about aging and what that means to you personally—how you use the time and capabilities that you have. We may want to interject thoughts about that—almost like little vignettes within a play, something where you pause and think about a specific thing.

I guess because I'm reaching a greater age, many aspects of the book make me reflect on aging itself.

Which, if we're lucky, everybody does.

Exactly. What we want to do with each chapter is make it easy for the reader at the very end, or when they come back to it later, to be able to contact either that person or what that person is involved in and see if they want to explore the cause further, if only on the internet. This book should be a real resource for anyone who is thinking about being an activist.

It's almost like a travelogue, where you can go and how you get there— because fortunately, we live in a time when so many people are usually able to do whatever they want. So many of us have paid our dues with obligations and responsibilities, and now that energy can be directed positively to some-thing that we believe in strongly.

Isn't the world lucky to have us elders! I think we should consider ourselves a gift in that sense. Not for the book. But each of the people in this book is a gift. Each reader is a gift. Anyone who is able to make the world better in some small way. There is no small way when you really think about it.

This provides one of the answers to the question, "What can I do about it?" That is something that I think energizes people and gives them the sense they're in control, that they've made a decision or choice, and they're going to make it (the cause) their own.

I think, in a very mundane sense, commitment to a cause relieves some of the frustration and anxiety that every thinking person is expe-riencing. Not just from personal challenges of aging, although that, too, but also from our knowing so much about what's going on in the world.

Whether we want to or not.

The thing is, people used to be able to choose *not* to know much more. We are no longer given that choice. The choice is not *whether* to know; it's what to know and believe.

Yes, you took the words right out of my mouth.

Well, that's good. We take the words right out of each other's mouths. That's why it's a partnership.

I really look forward to having this be the kind of book that lends itself to book clubs and discussion groups. This could be the vehicle to get groups brainstorming where you have a logarithmically improved idea bank.

I know we feel it's important to have a discussion guide in the book. We hope there will be groups who are moved to discuss their favorite character in the book. They are all real people, from different parts of the country, from different walks of life, and of different beliefs. They may differ in their hearts about many things, but they all are people we can admire for something they are doing about what they find needs doing.

One of the things I have realized through the interviews is the fact that if you put all our chapter people into a room, they probably would have some things they agree about and others they differ about, but they would always want to hear what each of them has to say. That openness seems to be a characteristic.

Yes, even in their causes. They are not so obsessed with what it is they are doing that they don't understand or listen to other people's points of view. Everyone we met seems to be open to what other people are doing and thinking about.

They've all agreed that we are going to tell the world about them. My daughter often reminds me that a real problem in society right now is that nobody wants to hear what the other side is thinking or saying or believing. Yet we have always been a country that had predominant philosophies, opinions, but we also found a way for people to live side-by-side with opposite views. In this time of change, taking responsibility for a decision to be an activist makes you realize you're setting your own course for change rather than having change imposed on you.

Yes. I agree that participation makes the adjustment to change easier.

The mindset here seems to be: "Here's what I believe, and here's what I am going to do. Do you feel like coming along?" You know, I am very big on choice, and the fact is that maybe some of these ideas and causes would not appeal to every person. But being able to appreciate what you read that a person has said and done, and giving them license to have those thoughts and take those actions, is certainly a peaceful way to live.

A constructive way! I think the readers can come away feeling that they've met some really interesting people they're happy to know and that, mostly, they didn't know about before. A few are better known than others, but for the most part, outside their own communities, or even inside their own communities, they are not well known. There are people here who might be their friends, given the opportunity. I hope knowing about them expands everyone's universe.

So do I. Because we have benefited from that expansion together—in so many ways that I would not have thought of before.

There is something wonderful about seeing how many different ways people express themselves and find passions to work through or about that are so creative.

All find creative problem-solving approaches. Because none of this "world-saving" is straight-lined. You get to one little corner, and you have to decide how to get around it. And the more you do, the easier finding your own resources becomes.

Well, I hope there are readers who feel better informed when they finish the book. I hope there are readers who will be diverted by the book. I hope some are amused by something they found. And I hope that some are inspired to do what these people did. But mainly, it's about all of us realizing that anybody can figure out something to do about something they see as a problem in our world.

Yes, because sometimes we get stuck in "if only." And knowing that you can turn that around and figure out just how! To me, that's empowering and surprisingly delightful.

As is doing this together. I think we should leave a very generous tip for our lovely server.

Introduction

$\mathcal{R}$emember when people used to talk about retirement? Have you noticed that the very word is fading? Losing its meaning? Losing the mental images it used to conjure, like the office party or the gold watch? We are in that fuzzy time when *retirement* sounds vague, but we haven't yet come up with its replacement. Perhaps, for the moment, at least, we might consider "*un*retirement" to signify the time when, traditionally, we leave the world of conventional employment or reach the age of collecting Social Security benefits. A career may have ended or been ended by a system that clings to old numbers—the ones that haven't yet been recalculated for changing demographics.

For most of today's people reaching yesterday's age of retirement, the days and years after are no different in terms of energy, smarts, or ability than the days before. In fact, the person on the "*un*retirement" side is probably smarter, abler, and certainly more experienced than he or she was the day before. The years that have gone before were a time of ups and downs, steps and missteps, and through it all, growth and development. The growth and development are still happening—with no definite end in sight, even as we begin to be aware of our own mortality. Still, the development of our interests, skills, and powers continues.

We, the authors, are not Pollyannas who see only rainbows where clouds threaten. We are not strangers to the many challenges living longer brings. Ageism is real. Loss of all kinds is real. And so is the challenge of living in this time real.

This is a time when the lengthening of life coincides with an explosion of change. Constant visual images and verbal memes crowd our sensibilities, bombard our psyches, overload our awareness of the political, spiritual, and geophysical upheaval shaking the institutions and values of the world we knew. Local crises and the possibility of worldwide catastrophe and are never far from our minds. Where we once were able to retreat quietly to enclaves of security, no place is now immune to the crushing load of information, misinformation, and disinformation that invades our lives, designed to manipulate our thoughts. Escape routes are closing fast.

Whether we want to or not, we know more about what needs fixing or who needs saving than any people who lived before us. Every gain in our ability to communicate has carried with it news of events bearing the underlying call: "HELP!" The call may also come from personal crises, such as illnesses and losses, that mark individual journeys through the years. We call the help chronicled in this book *activism*.

Who can come better prepared to activism than the *un*retired? As one of them, you know a lot about yourself, about everything you can, might, or think you should do. In fact, you know so much more than that. You've lived through growing older and growing up. You've made thousands of decisions, some little, and some dealing with circumstances you can't believe you weathered, and you've gathered wisdom along the way. You've learned to question and to think critically. You even have a good idea of what you know and what you don't know.

The people you will meet in these pages range in age from their early sixties to their mid-nineties. They tell us in their own words what they do and why they do it. They practice their activism alone or, more often, in groups. The social aspect is not the original impetus, although it often becomes a significant part of their lives. Volunteerism for its own sake is not what activism means to them, although many do regularly donate time, money, or service to other causes as volunteers. The activist's compelling goal, however, remains the same: *It (something) must be fixed—and I can do it or help!* A sense of urgency is invariably present.

It has been an honor to get to know the people in this book. Some have found themselves in leadership positions, but few began their activism with leadership in mind. The cause has been the thing, not their own positions among its advocates. From marching to improving road safety; from envelope-stuffing to making calls; from being arrested to circulating petitions; from fund-raising to letter-writing; from cooking in a community kitchen to starting an urban farm—for these people, it is not too late to try to save the world.

In a time when social media make shallow "clicktivists" of so many who hit "like" or select an emoji response to no measurable effect as they race through Facebook or Twitter, the people in this book are true activists. Some find that this new age and *un*retirement status brings a new perspective and results in the need to *do* more than to *say*. They tell us in their own words the what, why, and meaning of their activism. Time, for them, holds opportunity and urgency. Their passion and outlooks are fascinating and inspirational. For some, their activism provides one answer to the question, "Why am I (still) here?"

I

THE NEW SENIOR MOMENT

The people in this book change the meaning of "senior moment." The phrase is glibly tossed by people from thirty-five or forty on to describe a momentary lapse of memory. Can't think of someone's name? Uh-oh, it's a "senior moment." Forget where you put the keys? Likewise.

Was that a glimpse of future decline? Was it merely a funny toss-away line? Or was the forgetter whistling past the graveyard?

Calling those lapses "senior moments" reinforces the perception that everything about being "senior" is characterized by loss.

We love the fact that the people you meet here—and you, too—are redefining the term.

How about the realization that you just changed a life by befriending a child who needs a friend and role model? That's a "senior moment!"

What about the first time you were conscious of no longer being required to finish reading a book you really didn't like? Realized a person you had always avoided was interesting and could be a great friend? Understood that grief subsides and mourning ends?

Fill in all the examples you can think of; these are the true "senior moments." They are the moments when we realize our own growth, our own human development. They are what becoming a "senior" is all about.

The people in this book are living their "senior moments" as they continue to grow.

TR

Mignon S. Adams

COMMUNITY

$\mathcal{T}$he German sociologist Ferdinand Tönnies (1855–1936) defined community as "groupings based on feelings of togetherness."[1] He called it Gemeinschaft; the membership in this group was self-fulfilling. Mignon Adams grew up in small towns with that sense of community. When she was a young girl, her family moved from Oklahoma to Illinois, where the community was a close-knit group who knew each other well and shared the same values and conventions. During the 1970s she was involved in feminist activism. Mignon received all of her higher education, certification, and degrees from universities in Illinois. She earned a master's degree in library science.

She was accustomed to living and working in small college towns, where she enjoyed a vibrant social and cultural life. When she and her husband moved from Oswego, New York to Philadelphia, she served as director of Library and Information Services at the University of the Sciences for twenty-one years.

But the move initially had its social challenges. Mignon was used to a small, familiar group of friends and associates who shared activities in the bustling college towns where she had lived and worked. There were many cultural and informative events, activities that kept her connected and up to date. There was always something happening to explore—for entertainment, for learning, for fun. She found the transition to a city the size of Philadelphia "difficult." The sheer volume of opportunities and the extensive network of people spread

over a broad expanse meant she had to approach her desire for connection differently.

*I used to be able to jump in a car and drive to where I wanted to go. But
there were no driveways or individual garages. And the traffic! It certainly
was good to increase my walking abilities. Where was the yard to let the dog
out? Well, this was another good way to work on walking abilities.*

*In a small town, neighbors see you coming and going. But they don't
gossip about you.*

*Those you work with don't live close, so you don't see them outside of
work. Many things are more expensive in cities, like concerts; in small towns,
plays and performances are low in cost; parking is no charge.*

*But I've learned to get places without a car. I got to know other people in
other kinds of communities: church, clubs, etc. Walking was good for my health.
I took up volunteer ushering, and I choose more carefully what I attend.*

THE RISE OF AGING-IN-PLACE VILLAGES

In the latter part of the twentieth century, older adults often found
themselves in a dilemma. The desires and expectation of seniors, many
of whom were living alone, were very different from the generation that
came before them. For the first time, women, as well as men, had careers.
They were active and willing contributors to life in their society.

Among baby boomers, one of the catchphrases heard often is
"aging-in-place." You read about it in newspapers;[2] you get flyers sell-
ing services for it; you hear about it on the airwaves;[3] you even see it in
feature stories on television.[4]

As millions of us grow older, it is a concept that can be enticing.
In these modern, peripatetic times, kids, family, and friends scatter to
faraway places; we connect with phones and electronics. We don't want
to be a burden, and they don't want to feel guilty that we have needs.

Think of yourself making breakfast in your kitchen, or letting
your dog use that little door you had installed for her. If you need more
milk or oatmeal, you can go to the garage and take your own car to
the grocery store. If a summer concert strikes your fancy, you can call
friends from your house of worship or your neighborhood and arrange
an outing. And when your book club puts out a list of selections for the

coming year, you can get them from your local library. There are many features to being independent, and they bring a sense of comfort, purpose, and control.

But what happens if you lose some of your mobility, or your eyesight makes it dangerous to drive? What if death takes your beloved partner or family or friends? What if your day brings hours with nothing to do, no one to share a laugh? What if it does "take a village?" Research has shown that a sense of purpose, a self-perceived feeling of being useful, can contribute to a sense of connection in a community.[5]

In the past, traditional solutions might have included assisted living, nursing homes, continuous care facilities. Those options may not have much allure for twenty-first-century elders whose population numbers are growing significantly.[6] These adults have constructed lives of active intellectual engagement and varied lifestyle choices. As they age, independence is the key that helps to preserve their identity and stimulates further personal development. The many opportunities that come with being independent ensure that people are in charge of their own lives.

A solution to the problem is the idea of aging-in-place neighborhoods that tap into a valuable resource: other seniors. By banding together, seniors who live in the same community gain a support system and can pool the resources needed to acquire essential services.[7]

THE BEACON HILL MODEL

In 1999, a group of neighbors in the Beacon Hill section of Boston began discussing an arrangement that would allow them to live in their own homes as they grew older. They united to form a community in which they could rely on each other to be a support system. They combined their resources to avail themselves of essential services. These seniors became a nonprofit community, supported by annual membership dues that covered routine services. They identified offerings such as activities, transportation, dog walking, house cleaning, meal deliveries, technological training, and health services, such as visiting nurses and care managers. They decided to use the size of their group to bargain with vendors for discounted prices on purchases and services that were necessary.

The result was Beacon Hill Village, the first stay-at-home retirement "village." (Village refers to the community of members rather than a geographic location.) In 2002 the first members embarked on their grand experiment. Along the way, fifty-and-older members merged their experience and expertise to meet the practical challenges of living on their own. For instance, some who are lawyers, teachers, and tradespeople offered their skills to review legal documents, to teach language and computer classes, or to do household maintenance jobs. Many other opportunities presented themselves as the group grew, and members participated in the village.

The village hired an administrator and a few staff and set annual membership fees. Today, twenty years on, Beacon Hill Village is not only thriving but has become a model for the neighborhood-based village movement in the United States and around the world! Since then, hundreds of villages have opened, and many more are in development. These groups can have unique differences in organization and services that are designed to meet the needs of their membership. Indeed, there are many trends in senior living that are devised to answer most of the needs older people may have.[8]

To serve the expanding number of villages, Beacon Hill Village also helped to establish the Village-to-Village Network, "a national organization that collaborates to maximize growth, impact, and sustainability of individual Villages and the Village movement."[9]

FITC (PRONOUNCED *FIT'SEE*)

Such an organization took shape in 2010 in Philadelphia.

Friends in the City was the brainchild of four couples who wanted to retire in Center City [Philadelphia], to take advantage of its cultural riches, and have an instant band of compatriots with whom to socialize, volunteer, and look after one another.[10]

Friends in the City began testing the waters with a few members in a pilot program. They started a book club and an organized group for walking in the city. The first year was 2011. Thanks to the internet, FitC (fit'see), as it came to be known, increased to about fifty members. It operates in the tradition and values of the Society of Friends, whereby everyone has an equal vote. Decisions are not made by consensus. Instead, FitC is guided by the members' shared responsibility for the good of the group. Although it is a Quaker nonprofit, membership is open to all who apply. Today the FitC membership is more than 600, and there are forty different small interest groups. These are not cookie-cutter groups. Each group is free to organize and operate as the members choose.

After Mignon and her husband raised their family, he died in 2012.

FitC was in its first year when my husband died. After about three months, I wondered what I would do. Someone called and wanted to know if I'd serve on the oversight board (since I'm a Quaker and the board needed to be 50 percent Quakers). Along the way, someone mentioned there was a book group, so I went to a meeting, and someone else wanted to know if I'd do an event.

Mignon moved to a condo apartment in center city Philadelphia and became very active in FitC. Her shared goal in this endeavor is to "build a community in Philadelphia so that assisted living will be unnecessary." Unlike many other villages, FitC is a social group that provides many opportunities to live a healthy and pleasant life. She spends most of her time as one of the people who oversee the activities of Friends in the City.

Our goal is to have middle-class seniors feel as though they are part of a community where they can do things and go places to take full advantage of city living with people who have similar interests. There is also an information part because we share recommended service, professional, and tradespeople with whom we have been satisfied. There is often a list or a mention in the FitC online newsletter.

The Friends Foundation for the Aging provided a grant in 2010. Under its umbrella, there is also a residential option at Friends in the City—Riverfront; a personal services program available to FitC members called FitC Plus; or healthcare services with Friends LifeCare. Mignon is a board member of FitC.

Although her parents were Southern Baptists, Mignon is a member of the Society of Friends. She "found her own way" during the Vietnam years. She has also found gratification and lasting friendships while she strives to build the "community without walls" that is so valued by her and her peers.

HOW TO CONNECT!

The Age-in-Place Movement
  https://www.aarp.org/home-family/
Baltimore Yearly Meeting
  https://www.bym-rsf.org/who_we_are/organizations/friendshouse/
    friendshousereps.html
Beacon Hill Village
  https://www.beaconhillvillage.org/
Friends Center City (FitC)
  https://friendscentercity.org/
FitC Plus
  https://friendscentercity.org/content/fitc-plus-independence
    -convenience-peace-mind
Friends Center City—Riverfront
  https://friendscentercity.org/default/riverfront
Friends Journal
  https://www.friendsjournal.org/
Friends Services Alliance (formerly Friends Services for the Aging)
  https://www.fsainfo.org/
Kaiser Health News
  https://khn.org/
Quaker Aging Resources
  http://www.quakeragingresources.org/about-us/
SeniorAdvisor.com
  https://www.senioradvisor.com/blog/2019/05/15-senior-living-trends/
Senior Aging in Place
  https://www.aginginplace.org/
The Senior List
  https://www.theseniorlist.com/about-us/
Village to Village Network
  https://www.vtvnetwork.org/

Yoko Koike Barnes

UNEXPECTED FINDINGS

*D*estiny? Karma? Luck? How do you become the person you are today? The reflection required to answer that question can be enlightening, even surprising. For some, it's a puzzle. For others, it's a clearly defined path. That's how it is for Yoko Koike Barnes. Her life presented meaningful and relevant experiences, which made her the seventy-year-old activist she is today. Her mother was outspoken and encouraged her children to follow that model.

Yoko was born and raised in Tokyo as a Christian, a faith she says included just 2 percent of the Japanese population.

So I was used to being different. And I appreciate that our parents both encouraged us not to be afraid to be different. So that was a good thing that made a difference in my life. I always felt that my parents would have been behaving the way I was if they had lived in my time. Where conformity was the basis of society, my parents had encouraged us to be "different," especially my sister and me.

Yoko left Tokyo as a student when she was sixteen. Her first trip outside of Japan brought her to California for a year of high school in the 1960s. Her exposure to the burgeoning feminism in America had a dramatic impact. When she returned to Tokyo, she became an activist for the women's movement. She established one of the first women's rights groups in Japan. After college in Japan, while she was working, she became involved with other feminists. For seven years, she worked for the rights of women. This activism persisted as she tried to effect change in her workplace. At the same time, after their wartime defeat, many Japanese citizens were questioning the values in their social fabric.

When I was growing up, Japan went through enormous changes. It was an interesting time. Adults around us had lost confidence in their belief system. Before the war, they were told that the Emperor was God and that Japan was number one. They were in a state of shock during the years following the defeat in the war. We might say that my generation, born right after the war, took advantage of the chaos. Traditionally, the young would follow the paths of the elders, but those elders around us were "lost." We were given abundant freedom to explore new ideas.

It was a good place to be an activist. I was seeking how to go forward with my life when I was twenty-five to twenty-nine. Then I met someone from the States who came from this area [Philadelphia], and in the end, we got married here.

During the 1970s, she interacted with many Quakers in Philadelphia. Thus began a strong thirty-year guiding philosophy. Speaking up about women's issues, injustice, and inequality, and learning the Quaker tradition, she realized that even in the political movement, women were subjected to discrimination. And she found herself seeking meaning and a fuller life.

After being raised as a Christian, I started questioning the Christian religion. If you don't believe in Jesus and you won't be saved, what happens to 99 percent of the Japanese? So all these things combined and I left the Christian faith. But then I guess I was still searching. When I was ready, I became a Quaker, and I have been Quaker all my life since then. Being a Quaker feels like I have a quiet lake somewhere in myself I can go to.

She trained in activism at the Quaker Life Center. It was considered a radical group. They were determined to change the world. Individuals came from many parts of the United States as well as from other continents to learn nonviolent direct action. They focused on Vietnam War protests and "ism" injustices such as racism, sexism, etc. The members lived a communal life. At the Life Center, she was expected to work no more than twenty hours a week at an outside job. The rest of her time was to be dedicated to transforming the Life Center values into a system that could be lived and taught to others. Some people told her it was crazy to want to change the world. But she was undeterred.

All these people heard about this radical community where people can learn and be trained to be an activist, to change the world. For example, we had a car, and it was probably the first car share. We called it Old Blue, and somebody was in charge of taking care of it. But all the rest of us could borrow the car and use it. That was quite common in those days. Coming from Japan, that was quite a change.

Yoko had a respite after the Life Center training. Following a divorce, she raised her children for some years as a single mother. She earned a graduate degree. And then she married a second time, this time to a man who is a Quaker. She began an academic career as a Japanese language instructor at the University of Pennsylvania and then moved to the Haverford College faculty. She says that she reached stability in her life.

I was seeking something other than my work, other than my family, something that speaks to me. I knew there was something missing in my life. I knew it would be the time to find that something if I felt that way. So toward the end of maybe three or four years, I knew the next phase of life would bring me to what I was really seeking.

The focus of Yoko's activism changed in 2010. This was the year that she saw the documentary film, *The Dark Side of Chocolate*. The film recounts the experience of a European journalist who goes undercover to investigate the use of child slave labor. As an ongoing practice in West Africa, many of the cocoa bean farms exploit children to harvest the cocoa beans. This shocking realization awakened Yoko's need to be a part of the solution for this tragic problem.

Almost immediately, she found that there was a global movement addressing this issue. So she attended a national Fair Trade conference in Boston and brought her insights back to the Haverford campus. For two years she recruited and mentored college students to be Fair Trade activists in the fight for children's rights.

I was born so fortunate. I was fortunate all through the years, but it could have been me in those situations.

By 2013 Yoko had reached her planned retirement. She and her husband moved to an experimental, nonprofit, Quaker-inspired apartment building. It has residents from three generations. While aging in place, the older residents live cooperatively and share common interests. This was the perfect place for Yoko to use her newly available time to advance the cause of fair trade.

She helped to establish Fair Trade Philadelphia with a group of eight people. Although she hadn't considered being at the forefront, she reminded herself, "not to be afraid" to do it. Even though English is not her first language, she gives workshops, organizes activities, and speaks to children's groups at the Free Library. The children's program is called Nurturing Fair Minds. There have been cooking and shopping events. Participants can begin to familiarize themselves with the six logos on labels that identify Fair Trade products.

Often the producers of goods are marginalized, but the Fair Trade initiative aims to advocate for relationships between producers and consumers. Education of consumers is a primary goal. Yoko convinced the Philadelphia City Council to recognize the importance of fair trade and the efforts of Fair Trade Philadelphia. Her group identified the requisite sixty-one stores and restaurants that were using certified Fair Trade products. On October 15, 2015, the City Council passed the Fair Trade Resolution, which requires contracts to support Fair Trade principles, and Philadelphia became a Fair Trade city.

Today, the Fair Trade movement is a global network with hundreds of organizations in more than thirty-five countries.

Tell me, Yoko, how do you feel in terms of your life? You talked about thinking that you were seeking something. Now that you are doing this, what does it mean to you?

It only means what we make it mean so that work is now. It's not about me. I'm glad this is a forever project. It's not like "ok, you're done." Personally? I do feel full. I thought that I should carry on. I really see the meaning of my life to be with this.

These are the words I live by. They are not my own: to love one person as though to love the whole world, and to love the whole world as though to love one person.

I feel I was not given enough opportunities to get to know my father and vice versa. In his old age, my father told us he regretted his absence during our formative age.

In Japan, during the Edo period, 1603–1868, there was a caste system, Samurai on the top, then farmers, craftsmen, and then last were merchants. My mother used to say, with pride, that her children had all four in their heritage. My father's father was a craftsman, a furniture maker, and his wife came from a lower rank of Samurai. My mother's father was a farmer, and his wife was a merchant—making/selling Japanese sweets. Purity was not her pride—being mixed was.

HOW TO CONNECT!
Feature Length Films

About Bananas: *Beyond the Seal*
  http://beyondtheseal.com
About Chocolate: *The Dark Side of Chocolate*
  https://www.youtube.com/watch?v=15dJwA-xaVA
About Coffee: *After the Harvest-Fighting Hunger in the Coffeelands*
  https://www.youtube.com/watch?v=WbLlqle7mBw
About Fashion: *The True Cost*
  http://truecostmovie.com

Short Films

About Chocolate: *Why Fair Trade Chocolate Matters*
  https://www.youtube.com/watch?v=lnpsFRcsnE0
About Coconut: *Journey to Serendipol*
  https://www.youtube.com/watch?v=gtOQd748dC0&feature=youtu.be
About Fair Trade: *A Just World Starts with You*
  https://www.youtube.com/watch?v=xT6TQSxlDOY

Organizations and Websites

Equal Exchange
  http://shop.equalexchange.coop/
Fair Trade America
  http://fairtradeamerica.org
Fair Trade Campaign
  http://fairtradecampaigns.org/
Fair Trade Federation
  http://www.fairtradefederation.org/
Fair Trade International
  https://www.fairtrade.net/
Fair Trade Philadelphia
  http://www.fairtradephiladelphia.org. To receive the newsletter, send
    an e-mail to info@fairtradephiladelphia.org
Fair Trade Resources
  http://fairtradecampaigns.org/resources/
Fair Trade Town International
  http://www.fairtradetowns.org/
Fair Trade U.S.A.
  http://fairtradeusa.org/

Fashion Revolution
http://fashionrevolution.org/
Global Exchange
https://globalexchange.org/
The Good Trade
http://www.thegoodtrade.com/about-the-good-trade
Slave Free Chocolate
http://www.slavefreechocolate.org/
World Fair Trade Organization (WFTO)
http://wfto-asia.com/
http://wfto.com/about-us/history-wfto/history-fair-trade

Ashley Bryan

*Th*e oldest person in this book says that age is a number that is "absolutely meaningless." An acclaimed author and illustrator of children's books, he visited and spoke at the University of Pennsylvania in 2019. He was ninety-five.

It's the spirit of welcoming the day that makes all the difference. Because it's always a new day, like a new baby being born. Every day is an adventure in discovery. You're open to that. Always outreach to others; be aware that any outreach you do is meaningful to another. You don't know what they are going through. But the simplest thoughtful word or touch makes a big difference to them.

HOW DOES LIVING A LIFE IN A CERTAIN WAY SIGNIFY A "CAUSE"?

When we first learned about Ashley Bryan, we realized that it is in this very concept and action of "outreach" that he has so much to teach us as he continues to somehow improve the world. From his devoted nieces and nephews, to his many friends, to the countless readers, listeners, and eyes he has reached, to the casual visitors, always welcome to step through his open door and share a pot of tea, his reach enriches lives and will continue, through his example and his work, to do so for many years to come. It is true he was born with talent, but that was hardly enough by itself. As he says of having his first book (the first children's book written and illustrated by an African American author) published at forty, "Many were more gifted than I, but they gave up." Much more was involved in leading him to welcome each new day with so much appreciation and curiosity.

Through a world that could easily be viewed through a lens of limitations, including war and racism, his artist's lens has never stopped at himself. It has always included and reached out to others: family, students, children, neighbors. It began in the Bronx; it continues off the coast of Maine, on Great Cranberry Island, roughly two miles long by one mile wide, with a population of about fifty people year-round, and hundreds of daily visitors starting when spring breaks through.

When Ashley arrived at Great Cranberry Island about thirty years ago, a newly retired professor emeritus of art at Dartmouth, it was like coming home:

Life on the island is always a community, so it's what I live for. I feel wherever you live, you should create community so that you know each other in a family sense. That's the way this little island is. In the dead of winter, we have almost no visitors because the boat schedule is so irregular. There are a few things that bring us all together, like the neighborhood house and the library, where they have a coffee hour.

In New York, it was a lot like this, because we lived in tenement houses on the third or fourth floor, and we knew everyone in those houses, and everyone helped everyone. Moving to the island was, to me, like moving to a tenement house. When I arrived on the boat with my box of materials, someone reached for my box and passed it to another person and put it up onto the deck, so that was like my tenement house, so I'm home.

THE ROAD TO THE ISLAND

Ashley looks back on his earliest days as a beautiful time, filled with art and music and the birds his father, a greeting card printer, collected and nurtured. Although the 1930s were the time of the country's Great Depression, Ashley, like millions of others, benefited from the federal programs (the Works Progress Administration) that funded libraries and arts education. School was a place to learn how to draw, paint, and play musical instruments. The library fed his appetite for poetry, folk tales, and fairy tales. By seventeen, he was ready for art school. At Cooper Union, he was accepted on the merits of his work alone, judged in a blind test, and became the only African American student. Other schools had rejected him because of race.

Art school was interrupted by World War II and the draft. Ashley was among the segregated troops landing at Omaha Beach on D-Day (with his drawing pad stowed in his gas mask). After the war, and before he launched a career teaching art, Ashley completed his work at Cooper Union, attended graduate school at Columbia University, studying philosophy ("to understand war"), won a Fulbright Scholarship to the University of Marseille at Aix-en-Provence, and later studied at the University of Freiburg in Germany.

Before retiring to Great Cranberry Island, Ashley taught art at several schools and universities and began to create a whole genre of children's books that would delight and inspire children and their teachers and librarians.

SINCE "RETIREMENT"

"Retirement," in Ashley's case, refers simply to the time he moved from Dartmouth to Maine. It bears no resemblance to conventional notions of retirement. Since the 1980s he has been lauded for his books, appearances, and accomplishments that span paintings, literature, stage works, and collaborations with musicians that feature and celebrate his work. His awards can, and do, fill whole rooms. He considers his latest book, just completed, the "strongest, most beautiful work I have ever done." Libraries and literary festivals in the United States and Africa bear his name.

And yet, we particularly treasure Ashley Bryan as we write because of what his life, not his specific artistic accomplishments, tells us.

Any artist will tell us that her art is an expression of self. Skill and craft are taught, nurtured, developed. But the art is purely individual and belongs to the artist. When you talk with Ashley about his work and his life, they are one—and always expressed with the objective of his most frequently used word, "outreach." He may make a puppet, but it will be intended and used for the amusement of or exchange of ideas with a child. He loves to read his books and poetry to young audiences but does more than say the words; he expands the meaning with rhythm, gestures, and when he was younger, dance.

ASHLEY'S CAUSE

The objective is the same: that all of us, particularly as we age, can adopt a cause. One need not be an artist to emulate Ashley. The cause is to connect. To reach out. To listen. To respond. To be human.

At every moment I strive for connection. If you are in the moment, you are stretching out to reach that which you recognize in others. That's my secret.

HOW TO CONNECT!

Ashley Bryan Center
   https://ashleybryancenter.org/ashley.html

II

PLAY SOMETHING—ANYTHING

- An instrument (If you don't have one, get a harmonica—very good for breathing, too.)
- A comedy album
- Solitaire with an old deck of cards (even better than your iPad)
- Solitaire on your iPad
- A game with others
- Music for focused listening
- A part in a play
- With a toddler
- With a pet

*A*re you getting the idea? Can you enlarge that list with other examples of play in your life?

Play offers the same benefits for adults as it does for children. And it's almost as important in our development and in our emotional and mental health as it is in theirs. It needs to be part of our lives. It can be as exhausting as a team sport or as brief as telling or making a joke.

Play is serious business. *But not while you're engaged in it.* Its seriousness is measured only by its importance.

TR

· 4 ·

Rachna Mohaer Daryanani

FROM LUCKNOW, INDIA
TO MCALLEN, TEXAS

*W*hen Rachna (pronounced Rosh'na) Mohaer Daryanani first saw a refugee camp, it was not in McAllen. The first time she saw a refugee camp was when her father took each of his children to see where he and his family had been twenty years earlier, when India and Pakistan were partitioned. He impressed upon them that India was their country and had their loyalty although they had come from Pakistan and been displaced, but he also would never tolerate anti-Muslim slurs and always welcomed Muslims to their home.

In 1947, nearly twelve million people were displaced along religious lines, separating the two areas into the Dominion of Pakistan (majority Muslim), now the Islamic Republic of Pakistan, and the Dominion of India (majority Hindu), now the Republic of India. Not being Muslim, Mr. Mohaer's family were uprooted from their homes and sent to a refugee camp before settling in Lucknow and eventually in Calcutta, where Rachna was raised and her family prospered.

Rachna came to the United States in 1984, when she was thirty years old, and raised her son and daughter here. In 2018, she saw her second refugee camp (detention center) in McAllen, Texas, where she arrived tired from her bus journey with the Grannies Respond Caravan that started in Beacon, New York.

THE CHILD BECOMES THE GRANDMOTHER

Rachna's musical voice and warm, smiling demeanor are evidence of a presence that has surely been appealing always to children as well as to her contemporaries as she has grown. As a child whose first language was Sindhi, she became fluent also in Bengali and English, attending a Catholic school along with her older siblings. She was aware from her earliest days both of her family's privilege and the disparity between her own secure life and that of others.

We had a rickshaw driver who took us to school every day. The other family members would never talk to him, but I knew his name and about his family. I am and was always a chatterbox. My grandmother made lunch every day. My older sisters were given money to spend at school, and one day I asked my sister if she would give me money for lunch as I didn't like the lunch I had. When she did, the driver asked me if he could have the lunch that I didn't want because he didn't have food for his children. I couldn't eat that day. I couldn't sleep.

I talked it over with my mother. She made a plan with me, just between us, to help him. I said, "Give me double food so I can give him half." It would have to be our secret. Then my mom went one step further. She is a very educated woman. She told the driver to bring his children and leave them at our house for his two-hour rounds. It had to be our secret; otherwise, everyone would discuss it and have different opinions. She would feed them.

We always had the custom of teaching those children and servants' children, of passing on our books. We had to do our handwritten lessons carefully as they were passed on to students who followed us. I hope they're doing well!

Rachna's instincts and the customs and attitudes learned as a child are hardwired in the grandmother she has become, and the causes on which she has focused her activism, even as she has straddled different continents and different cultures.

A WOMAN IN INDIA

I was always getting into trouble because I was considered too independent. My parents were against my going to law school, as I desired. [BTW: Rach-

na's daughter is an attorney.] So it was nursing school for me. I was blamed there for starting a riot among the students. When I became ill and was sent to the hospital, other students demonstrated because I was put in a general ward instead of a private room. As a nursing student, I had grumbled to some of the doctors that I was upset that they didn't treat me as "one of the family." That put an end to my nursing career before it started. The school no longer wanted me. I "caused strife," in their words.

So I did enter law school—one of three girls in the school. One of the professors would never call on me. Once I stood in the back of the class and refused to sit down. The professor said, "You're supposed to take a seat!" I said, "You're supposed to treat all students equally." He said, "I decide who gets the question." I said, "I decide whether I know the answer or not. I'm just raising my hand to tell you I know the answer. I'm not telling you to call on me." After that, all the boys in the class used to come and take lessons from me. I was a horror! But I loved every minute of it.

Father would say, "What is wrong with those boys? Must they find a girl to teach them?"

Rachna's independence was limited, however. Her law school days ended before completion with the arranged marriage to the son of her father's best friend. Time was spent assuming responsibility at home while her husband went first to Surinam and then to New York, establishing the family's jewelry business.

ACTIVISM

Rachna's work as an activist/volunteer is characterized by her seeing a need and filling it. This is borne out by her experience with the VA and Grannies Respond.

The VA

At the VA hospital in her area, Rachna visited, walked with, and talked with veterans, and accompanied them on day trips. She also read to people and soon realized that some would surely benefit from reading stories together. She started with newspapers, but expanded the readings to books or stories, some of which she, or willing readers, read aloud. Her sensitivity to her audience made it clear that while the comprehension and social benefit of the experience was for everyone, some lacked the ability or confidence to read aloud. She became a vital part of the institution, eventually also answering their request to take over the running of the gift shop.

Grannies Respond

Along with many others, Rachna has been moved by the plight of children and their mothers caught in the confusion and trauma of what awaited them at the borders as they sought refuge in the United States from violence at home. America! "The Gates of Hope" would surely be open to them. When Rachna learned of the newly formed group called "Grannies Respond/Abuelas Responden," she determined to join in their caravan from the Northeast to the border town to assess the asylum-seekers' situation and see how they might help.

The organization's mission is to provide compassionate and respectful support to immigrants seeking safety and security in the United States. Among other services, they send volunteers to bus stations in cities across the country to greet asylum seekers and provide them with basic necessities they need to get them to their next stops. This "Overground Railroad Project" has grown to more than eight cities. They also send volunteers to the border to assist asylum seekers and help with resettlement work. Their stated plan is always to "provide a smiling and a caring face."

Rachna left on her birthday, July 31, 2017, for the ten-day journey with two vans filled with fifteen people, fourteen of whom were strangers, eventually meeting buses with more than 200 more. The strangers became not only friends, but family. When they stopped overnight, they were met by volunteers at a church. A ninety-four-year-old woman greeted Rachna and took her to her home.

She drives and lives alone. We met at 9:00 p.m., and I had to be back at 6:00 a.m. She was a Holocaust survivor. We talked until 3:00. And when I left, she had packed a breakfast for me.

In McAllen, we stayed in hotels and divided into groups. We were not allowed to enter the detention center but went to a large area covered with a blue tarp. We observed and found what we could do. I soon real-

ized that mothers, few of whom spoke English, were holding their babies and toddlers close. No one seemed to understand them. Many, Hondurans and Guatemalans, had different dialects. Through gestures and sign language, I learned that they were afraid to leave to go to the bathroom. As I convinced first one and then another, I got them to leave their children with me and feel safe enough to go. So there I was, with one on my lap and others gathering around me. I was playing, I thought, while others are working!

Playing, of course, was exactly what was needed. Mothers were afraid to leave their children. Some, as Rachna later learned, had heard of children being snatched from their mother's arms and taken off, perhaps, they heard, for adoption or placement where the mothers would never see them again.

When Rachna left McAllen, her next step would be to study Spanish so she could be of more help. From aging and wounded veterans to frightened mothers and babies, Rachna's sensitivity, humor, kindness, and musical voice change their worlds when she is present.

UPDATE

Having recovered from a recent illness, and with her doctor's admonition against flying, Rachna has been given his go-ahead to travel instead by bus to Miami, Florida for the June Father's Day protest against family separation of newly arrived asylum seekers. She contacted a few fellow travelers who share her commitment to the children living in reportedly unpleasant, unsafe, and sometimes terrifying conditions and arranged to meet a few in New Orleans before going on together. She plans to arrive early to visit and help the children and mothers as much as she is able or allowed.

Rachna has asked her grandchildren, who are eight and thirteen years old, to write letters she will bring to the children, assuring them that there are people who care about them here. She is asking her Boy Scout grandson to find out if she might visit his troop and tell them about where she is going and why. She will return in time for her early July doctor's appointment.

HOW TO CONNECT!

Article Twenty Network
   http://www.a20n.org
Families Belong Together
   https://www.familiesbelongtogether.org/
Grannies Respond
   www.granniesrespond.org
Humanitarian Respite Center in McAllen, TX
   https://www.catholicextension.org/new-home-humanitarian-respite
   -center-mcallen
Lawyer Moms of America
   https://lawyermomsofamerica.squarespace.com/
VA Voluntary Service
   https://www.volunteer.va.gov
Veterans Service Corps
   https://www.vscamerica.org/

Beth Dolan

$\mathcal{B}$eth Dolan didn't give much thought to post-traumatic stress disorder (PTSD) until 2013.

I hosted a radio show, a podcast called Being Deliberately *on BlogTalk Radio from our production studio, Coyote Pass Productions in Altadena, California. It featured the stories of inspired people doing inspiring things in the world. I met a woman, a civilian, whom I interviewed twice for the podcast. She was working with the military at Camp Pendleton. She told me about PTSD and the great need for mental health awareness and reform in the military. I really didn't know anything about it. Two of my brothers were West Point graduates who had served in the military during peacetime, and my sister married a friend of theirs, a West Point classmate on active duty. But none of them had ever experienced the kind of trauma that could cause PTSD. This woman was desperate to do something for the returning vets. And she asked me what I would do if I wanted to help. My response was that I would probably make a film about it.*

Beth was prepared to make this happen. She has years of experience as a writer and producer. After graduating from Carnegie Mellon, Beth worked in the theater in New York. She and her husband, Luis Remesar, also a writer and producer, moved to Los Angeles to transition to film and television.

HER LEARNING CURVE

The year was 2013, a time when the discussion of military mental health was still "in the back room." She researched intensely and was shocked by what she learned.

In 2007, the Department of Defense (DoD) Task Force on Mental Health was convened by mandate of Congress to assess and make recommendations about mental health services available to members of the armed forces. There were four "interconnected" goals for those services: a culture of support for psychological health and to dispel stigma; a full continuum of excellent care; allocation of sufficient and appropriate resources; visible and empowered leadership. They arrived at a single finding "underpinning all others: the Military Health System lacks the financial resources and the fully-trained personnel to fulfill its mission to support psychological health."[1]

The facts Beth found in her research reinforced her decision to make a social justice documentary film. By August 2014, the commitment to production was firm. Her film was going to bring attention and reform to the problem of military mental healthcare. She called it *Stranger at Home* because that is a succinct description of the feeling of many returning combat veterans struggling to make the transition back to "normal" life.

We [she and her husband, Luis Remesar] set the intention to find the right people at the highest level in the military to provide us with the facts.

One of Beth's consultants is Mark C. Russell, PhD, ABPP, a retired US Navy commander who served as a military clinical psychologist for more than twenty-six years. A veteran of Operation Enduring Freedom in Afghanistan and Operation Iraqi Freedom, Dr. Russell was called to testify before the task force regarding his efforts to prevent a military mental health crisis. He is an advocate for a Behavioral Health Corps in the armed services, similar to medical, dental, veterinary, legal, and supply corps, thus affording mental health equal status and priority as physical health.

After retiring from the navy, Dr. Russell established the Institute of War Stress Injuries, Recovery, and Social Justice at Antioch University–Seattle. He chairs the PsyD (Doctor of Psychology) program in the School of Applied Psychology, Counseling, and Family Therapy. The institute trains professionals to deal with wartime behavioral health crises and is a center for research.[2]

IMPACT

Beth met with individual veterans; veterans' groups; two front-line experts: a navy psychologist and a marine psychologist; a veteran of

Vietnam; and mental health professionals to explore their data and solicit their recommendations. In the film's trailer, there is commentary from retired army ranger Steven Elliot, a friend of Pat Tillman, also a ranger. Steven was caught in the firefight in which Tillman was killed by friendly fire, chronicled in the book *Where Men Win Glory*[3] and the film *The Tillman Story*.[4] Shannon McGraw, a Marine Corps veteran and Marine Corps Judge Advocate (attorney), talks about being a warrior, protecting her son. She eloquently describes her own PTSD as a veteran and single parent: "I come to the table a little bit broken."[5]

That was six years ago. Today, the campaign is more compelling than ever because a national conversation about military mental health is evolving. It has been brought into public awareness as an imperative.

FAR-REACHING EFFECTS

The consequences of PTSD can reverberate among families, friends, even communities. A crisis can arise that devastates entire families. Suicide is just one of the possible outcomes. In the January 1, 2019, online issue of *Military.com*, Patricia Kime reported that at 2018 year-end "57 active-duty deaths represent a 25 percent increase from 2017, the highest number of suicides since the service began closely tracking them in 2001."[6]

The US military finished 2018 with a troubling, sad statistic: It experienced the highest number of deaths by suicide among active-duty personnel in at least six years.

Army spokeswoman Colonel Kathleen Turner validates the necessity for action. She told *Military Times*, "While the Army has made progress, more work needs to be done." Meanwhile, in 2018 statistics show that the Marine Corps reported its highest suicide numbers in ten years.[7] According to Military.com, in 2018 the total active-duty reports of death by suicide across the four DoD services are the highest they've been since 2012, which had been the DoD services' worst year since it began centrally tracking reports in 2001.[8]

"We must continue to ensure commanders have the policies and resources they need to prevent suicides, that all leaders have the tools to identify soldiers who are suffering and to positively intervene, and that all soldiers view seeking mental health care as a sign of strength," Turner said.[9]

DIFFERENT THERAPIES IN TREATING PTSD

Neurofeedback, a recent therapy, is offered through the EEG Institute in Woodland Hills, California. Clients can achieve improved self-regulatory capacity and mental functioning with the aid of neurofeedback. Neurofeedback is "exercise" for the brain. It is a gradual learning process by which a person learns to change their brain waves and thereby gain better control over their brain states.[10]

Also offered at EEG Institute is recovery from trauma. Homecoming for Veterans is a national outreach program to provide cost-free neurofeedback training for veterans as part of the rehabilitation of PTSD and issues of brain performance. The Institute has formed partnerships with more than twenty other organizations that support their work.[11]

Another kind of therapy in use is eye movement desensitization and reprocessing (EMDR), which combines exposure therapy with a series of guided eye movements that help to process traumatic memories and change how a person reacts to them.

THE BOTTOM LINE

Today Beth is just as committed to the project as she was when she began. Funding and finishing *Stranger at Home* has become the cause of her life, a mission that has her absolute dedication.

The element that slows her down is getting more funding. While she searches for revenue sources, her goal is to do everything she can to keep the discussion alive, in front of the public as a priority.

Beth told me,

I want to contribute to the transformation of military mental health practices and policies. My greatest wish is that the conversation about mental health and mental health reform will become spotlighted and stigma-free forever.

Through all the obstacles she has had to surmount in these five years, Beth Dolan has shown her mettle, proven her authenticity, and demonstrated her tenacity. Now in her early sixties, she has used all her resources to expose and document the records of lives damaged and altered by our enemies. The question Beth has for each of us is:

Will we stand with those to whom we owe our utmost loyalty?

HOW TO CONNECT!

The Armed Services YMCA
https://www.asymca.org/

Department of Defense Task Force on Mental Health. *An Achievable Vision: Report of the Department of Defense Task Force on Mental Health*. Falls Church, VA: Defense Health Board, 2007.
https://archive.org/stream/AnAchievableVisionReportOfTheDepartment OfDefenseTaskForceOnMental/MHTF-Report-Final_djvu.txt p ES-4

EEG Institute
Find a local provider at http://www.homecoming4veterans.org/

Final Salute Inc.
https://www.finalsaluteinc.org/Home.html

Fisher House
https://www.fisherhouse.org/

From the Heart Productions
https://fromtheheartproductions.com

Give an Hour
https://giveanhour.org/

The Intrepid Fallen Heroes Fund
https://iava.org

Justice for Vets
https://justiceforvets.org/

Make the Connection
https://maketheconnection.net/

National Military Family Association
https://www.militaryfamily.org/

Operation Home Front
https://www.operationhomefront.org/

The Semper Fi Fund
https://semperfifund.org/

Team Red White and Blue
https://www.teamrwb.org/

Thank You for Your Service
https://www.amazon.com/gp/video/detail/0IV7629KC1DFB3D6A8U GN6LJIS/ref=imdbref_tt_wbr_piv?tag=imdbtag_tt_wbr_piv-20

Pat Tillman Foundation, Tillman Scholars
https://pattillmanfoundation.org/meet-our-scholars/

The Tillman Story
https://www.amazon.com/Tillman-Story-Pat/dp/B004LFEK06

U.S. VETS
https://www.usvetsinc.org/programs-services/

Vietnam Veterans of America
https://vva.org/

III

CONTR_ _ VS. CONTR_ _ _ _ _

FILL IN THE BLANKS AND IDENTIFY THE VERBS!

Hint: If You Want to Fix the World and You Are (Sigh) a Mere Mortal, Think about the Difference

*O*ne makes me feel powerful. I definitely know best. I'll make it happen. I'll stop it/her/him/them.

One makes me part of something. It is likely to require cooperation, tact, even humility to effect change and affect outcomes.

You've got it! The verbs are "control" and "contribute."

CONTROL

One of life's most important lessons is knowing how little we control—outside ourselves, that is. In fact, it turns out that our selves are the only things we do control. Even the individual humans and animals that we raise and nurture are beyond our control. We can help them survive and thrive through our support in all kinds of ways, but control is beyond our power. They, too, each have a self. As to events outside ourselves, even the most threatening—the ones that really happen and the ones we fear may happen—the realization that by ourselves we are powerless to control them is eventually followed by anxiety, anger, and frustration in the face of our helplessness. A positive outcome, however, is found by many through banding with others—becoming activists.

CONTRIBUTE

I have so much to give! Every idea and ideal, every cause and effort that speaks to my heart and intellect can benefit from my personal action. Most amazing is knowing that I'll never know effects I may have on others. Once in a great while, a young person may tell you, "I never forgot what you said to me," but that's just the icing on the cake of life.

TR

· 6 ·

Peggy Ellertsen

ARE YOU LISTENING?

*U*ntreated hearing loss is one of the most emotionally crippling impairments. It can affect every aspect of a person's life. Isolation, depression, retreat from the uncomplicated and spontaneous communications that guide and enrich our lives—these are a few of the results that a person might experience. Peggy Ellertsen saw this firsthand. Her mother lost her hearing when Peggy was young, and with it came her sad and unexpected transformation.

My mother was a quietly dazzling woman. She was a great and wonderful mother. She was very kind, very emotionally generous, particularly when I was a young child, through my elementary school years. She was a reliable friend and a wonderful coach. She had strong friendships. She was not someone I would describe as dynamite, just a quiet presence. She was fully engaged in life. Then as she began to lose her hearing, she began to lose her Self.

She would describe her hearing loss as a result of having diphtheria as a child. Later I learned that it was very likely not the cause because my grandfather had a severe hearing loss too. I think she wanted to protect me, to save me from worry about my own hearing.

As her impairment progressed, she became exhausted, trying to listen really hard. She became very emotionally dependent on my father. She gave it everything she had, but in the end, it was too much for her. It [the progression of the hearing loss] was very painful for her. It was also painful for me to witness her decline. I've always thought that because of the way it played out, it contributed to her ultimate cognitive decline. I think of her as someone who died of hearing loss. Sometimes people are shocked when I say that.

In Peggy's mother's time, there was a terrible stigma associated with hearing loss, and Peggy believes that the stigma held her mother back from conventional engagement in her world. Unfortunately, it also heightened her sense of isolation.

Sometimes stigma is external. Hearing loss is often associated with smugness or aging or infirmity, but you get the sense that there are these clear prejudices. Sometimes the stigma comes from within the person who feels diminished. They may feel less and less intelligent, less sharp.

ONSET

When Peggy went off to college, the memory of her mother's painful times was always in her mind.

I was very interested in the Communication Disorders department, so when I had to declare a major, I became a speech pathology major. It established a very important connection that bore a lot of fruit later on because speech pathologists deal with a whole range of communication disorders. For my entire work life, I was involved in working with students with language disabilities, kids with literacy problems, and those with written language needs.

By Peggy's last semester in college, her mother had lost almost all of her hearing.

Then during my senior year, just before graduation, my department head in the Speech and Language Department acquired new and sophisticated audiological testing equipment. The chair of the department asked the graduating seniors to step up as volunteers in a pilot program where he would work with the new technology.

He tested my hearing, and he ran all the tests. Afterward, he sat me down, and he said that I had mild sensorineural hearing loss. I had no idea that my hearing was not within the normal range. Of course, I freaked out because I sort of knew what it was going to mean for me.

I got hearing aids right away even though I probably could have gone for a long time hiding it. I hated the sound of them; I hated the feel of them; I hated the fact that I knew absolutely no one besides my mother and my grandfather, not to say anyone my own age who had hearing loss.

SURMOUNTING BARRIERS

Peggy tried the hearing aids for months, but she found that using them was very stressful. With that prolonged and negative encounter behind her, she put them in a drawer until she was in her thirties when she moved to Boston for graduate school. All that time, as she worked with elementary schoolchildren, she was attentive to the status of her hearing loss. After testing second graders with a portable audiometer, she would go back to her office and check her own hearing "almost as a preoccupation." Finally, she got better hearing aids and also came to accept that her hearing loss was something to live with, to manage. Acceptance seemed to be the way, finally, to get comfortable with the impairment.

DECISIONS, RESOURCES, TURNAROUND

Becoming a mother was also a turning point for Peggy.

It became clear to me that I wanted to change my mother's story. I wanted to set an example for my children. I didn't want them to see me as a burden. I wanted them to see me as able to take care of myself.

Still, her invisible condition advanced. She couldn't go to the movies anymore. She didn't hear the punch line of jokes.

I felt things slipping away. I began to disclose to clients, friends, and extended family members that I had a hearing loss.[1] Then I discovered the Hearing Loss Association of America (HLAA). It was a game changer—in fact, a lifesaver. That's when, I swear, the good fortune in my life really kicked in.

Mine was a typical reaction like others who find HLAA. Suddenly you are among a group of high-functioning people who have the same disability that you do. There is a ton of information and many educational opportunities to learn about the disability; to learn what you need to do to have a good outcome. Whatever the reason, so much of this information is not in the [general] pipeline of hearing loss.

That is the reason I do what I do. And I do a lot of it.

Peggy's younger daughter was diagnosed with a complicated hearing loss as a child, and she was fitted with hearing aids, which she sometimes color-coordinated with her outfit. But by the time she went to high school, she no longer needed them. She is very mindful about her hearing, using protective earplugs during loud noise exposure, and remains vigilant about her hearing.

OPENING INFORMATION HIGHWAYS

Peggy worked as a speech and language pathologist and a reading and language specialist in clinic, public school, and private practice settings for more than thirty years.

Now through HLAA, Peggy presents workshops, sometimes with her colleagues, to help clients solve problems with hearing loss like developing practical strategies to work around stigma.

The strategies she encourages help to build a healthy response to feelings of exclusion, however unintentional they may be, and to be able to self-advocate in social situations. Age-related hearing loss is the third most prevalent condition in older adults. An untreated hearing loss often results in changed relationships. Peggy wants these teachable strategies to be part of hearing healthcare, which can be introduced earlier than has been usual following the diagnosis of hearing loss. Armed with hopeful and up-to-date information, people can transition to the use of technologies sooner.

It may not occur to a person without a hearing impairment, but it is noteworthy to say it can have a direct effect on relationships.

The social contract changes because you are asking the speakers in your life to do something that's fundamental (conversation) in a very different way. You're asking them not only to have a conversation but to slow down their delivery or to be aware of the importance of not speaking over another person because that always creates a communication barrier.

If you have a significant hearing loss, and you're asking people to do things in a way that they normally wouldn't do, some people buy in, and some people don't. So the person with a hearing loss often begins to develop coping skills around these problems and starts to make opportunities that sometimes turn out well and sometimes don't.

HEARING LOSS HEALTHCARE

The vision of the American Speech-Language-Hearing Association (ASHA) is making effective communication, a human right, accessible and achievable for all. In 2003, Peggy "crossed over" to ASHA's Special Interest Group for Aural Rehabilitation and Its Instrumentation for adults with acquired hearing loss. Aural rehab is a deep and immersive treatment that goes far beyond just wearing hearing aids. It is a person-centered approach to the assessment and management of hearing loss.[2] Peggy is a student of best practices in aural rehab.

The percentage of senior citizens with hearing loss who use technologies, hearing aids, who self-advocate now is roughly 20 percent. For the other 80 percent, some of that has to do with the cost. But it also means that some people would like to pretend they can hear.

Aural rehab uses devices that have to do with exploiting the benefits of hearing aids by using assistive technologies, such as induction loop systems in large group areas, text telephones (TTY, TDD), and alerting devices that use lights or vibrations, to name a few.

There are a number of situations where my assistive devices make all the difference for me. For example, I take a yoga class one or two times a week, and my teacher uses my assistive devices.

I go to yoga because hearing loss is extremely stressful. Staying engaged is very important, which just happens to be the subject of studies that are being done on (so-called) Blue Zones on the planet. Blue Zones are six areas on the earth, such as Loma Linda, California, where people have healthy rates of longevity with strong cognitive ability and a strong sense of well-being. Scientific studies are being conducted into the lifestyle of people who live in these zones. It is fascinating! One of the things continually mentioned is the significance of engagement. We know now that engagement is highly correlated with well-being, particularly as a person gets older. It is also so very important with hearing loss.

Peggy is enthusiastic about all the brain research that is being conducted today. Of particular interest is the possible connection between untreated hearing loss and the development of dementia in the elderly, which is being explored at Johns Hopkins University.

She has published in the *Journal of the Academy of Rehabilitation Audiology*, coordinates the Boston chapter of the HLAA Speaker and

Workshop series, and has developed their website as a resource base. In addition, Peggy maintains a small private practice in the Boston area. She works closely with communities and businesses to make the world more accessible and enjoyable to people who have hearing loss.[3]

At seventy-two, Peggy welcomes each day as an opportunity to spread the current resources and evidence-based practices about hearing loss management to everyone she can help. Her zeal gives momentum to her extraordinary drive.

HOW TO CONNECT!

AARP: Hearing Loss Linked to Dementia
https://www.aarp.org/health/brain-health/info-07-2013/hearing-loss
-linked-to-dementia.html
American Academy of Rehabilitative Audiology
https://www.audrehab.org/
American Speech-Language-Hearing Association
https://www.asha.org/PRPSpecificTopic.aspx?folderid=8589943779&
section=Resources
Blue Zones
https://www.bluezones.com/
Gallaudet University
Laurent Clerc National Deaf Education Center
https://www3.gallaudet.edu/clerc-center/info-to-go/national
-resources-and-directories/national-conferences-and-exhibits.html
Hearing Loss Association of America
https://www.hearingloss.org/
The Johns Hopkins Bloomberg School of Public Health
https://hub.jhu.edu/2018/03/01/johns-hopkins-cochlear-center-for
-hearing-loss/
https://www.hopkinsmedicine.org/health/conditions-and-diseases/
hearing-loss/audiology
National Center for Biotechnology Information
U.S. National Library of Medicine
https://www.ncbi.nlm.nih.gov/

Leonard Finkelstein

FROM WORK TO PASSION

When does a job or profession become a cause? When does earning a living turn into a calling? The answer might be "never" for most of us. For the fortunate, it happens almost immediately, to the lifelong benefit of the one who is called, and to the benefit of countless others, most of whom he or she will never know. This is what happened when Leonard Finkelstein was discharged from the US Army in 1953 at the age of twenty-four. He decided to go directly to graduate school at Temple University to earn his doctoral degree in education. He knew he would find opportunity for work to support his young family: a wife who was a teacher, and four children. It proved to be a springboard to a life of creativity, collaboration, service, and intellectual stimulation that continues to this day.

Starting as a science teacher, Leonard's professional portfolio quickly expanded to include working with other teachers as he became a principal by his early thirties. Then he assumed the role of trouble-shooter as an auxiliary principal in more than thirty schools. Next, he became a district superintendent. Finally, he spent ten years as the superintendent of schools in Cheltenham Township, Pennsylvania, a district where the three superintendents who preceded his tenure had lasted for alarmingly brief periods. In this rapid rise, Leonard's focus was always on improving the lives and learning of kids and the collaboration and development of the professionals who taught them.

ROOM FOR CREATIVE
THINKING AND INNOVATION

Leonard saw that there was opportunity in education for creative solutions to problems and for innovation in programs. He introduced a core curriculum in his early days of teaching and was a founder of the Parkway Program in Philadelphia. This was a famed "school without walls" that enlisted the participation of corporate and nonprofit institutions and local colleges and universities to provide instruction and mentoring for high school students who could benefit greatly from its "out-of-the-box" approach to learning. This open-minded and open-hearted approach to education marked Leonard's ability to appreciate the work of others and to collaborate on projects as he consulted far from his home base in Pennsylvania.

Let's let Leonard tell us about this in his own words:

When I knew we'd be talking, I started making some notes—not in any particular order. There's been so much! I was a treasurer on the board of the World Council for Gifted and Talented Children, so I traveled to many countries, doing programs for gifted and talented children. All of a sudden, I was invited by the Aramark Company to organize their food services in Indianapolis for the Pan-American Games. It was different and fun for me, but while I was in Indianapolis, I saw people I knew from my work back east in education, and they asked me to coach some principals and superintendents who were having problems. The Eli Lilly Foundation is there, and they asked that I work with their education arm, which led to more traveling.

In Thailand I did a presentation and a woman sitting on a sofa sent someone over to tell me that she would like me to travel to other parts of the country and work with students in those places. Then, in China, while I was working with people for three weeks, I was told, "We've made arrangements for you to go to this city and this part of China and another part of China." Leila, my wife, and I have traveled a great deal, but never in this way before—nor with the opportunities for work and relationships we enjoyed. In one city in the far west of China the teacher had a hundred and thirty kids in her room and was doing such a fine job. She was preparing them for an exam. When I talked to her afterward, I said, "How do you do this? This is magnificent." And she said, "Well, I have a hundred and thirty kids, but I only have that one class during the week, so I can concentrate on all of them, and any kid that is having a problem I can work with separately." It was just a different format that I had never seen before, and she was so brilliant for being able to do all of that.

Wherever Leonard went, he not only inspired others with his coaching and example; he appreciated the work of those he met. This led to his involvement with other leading educators and businesspeople who formed a group called "Educational Insights." (This is not related to the for-profit business by the same name.) Under its aegis and shared commitment to bring educational change for the better, Leonard traveled widely.

It was fabulous. From a talk in Portugal to a meeting in a hostel in Chile. And then Lehigh University and the Princeton Center for Leadership Training. We just went nonstop, and in each instance Leila and I were able to do something significant for some of the people there to give them ideas that would help.

A CULMINATION

The Educational Insights experience led Leonard to establish the nonprofit organization called Global Youth United (GYU), which he directed until several years ago. GYU works in dozens of schools in Philadelphia with the cooperation of the University of Pennsylvania. The high school students, all volunteers, identify and research social problems around the world.

I would start them out with an overview of what GYU means (the motto is "Inspire, Empower, Change") and tell them, "Go out and do it! No teachers, you're in charge. A teacher can be there, but it's your baby!" And the ideas they came up with—and still do—were amazing. We're donating money we raised to their high schools for their recognition at graduation.

Leonard stepped back from the running of GYU, but remains committed to its work, to his Central High School Alumni Board, and his expanding interest in Whole Brain Education, a subject on which he has lectured widely. He is planning to put together a program on whole brain approaches to living a more joyous life.

Dr. Finkelstein's birthday is December 31. This ensures, he says, that every year a big celebration takes place, including the New Year's fireworks he and his family can see from their balcony facing the Philadelphia Art Museum. He and the many thousands whose lives he has touched have much to celebrate.

AUTHOR'S NOTE

When I arrived at Dr. Finkelstein's home, he had been writing a letter. He and his wife had just returned from a long weekend in New York, during which they had taken a three-hour boat ride on the river to view and learn about the architecture visible from the boat. He was writing to the representative of the architectural group that sponsors the tours about the guide's performance. Ever the teacher, critical observer, and coach, he was telling the guide (a) how ineffectual his presentation was and why several listeners left to go outside and avoid the lecture after one hour, and (b) detailed suggestions on how to make the experience interesting and meaningful for both the listeners and the guide himself. Ever true to his calling!

HOW TO CONNECT!

Eli Lilly Foundation
  https://lillyendowment.org/
World Council for Gifted and Talented Children
  https://world-gifted.org/

Bob Groves

GOING GLOBAL

*N*othing in his quiet, serious demeanor or direct, interested gaze suggests the fierce inner drive of the determined activist sitting across from me, speaking so quietly. Bob Groves, who had never taught before, created the always over-subscribed Human Rights in the 21st Century course at OLLI (Osher Lifelong Learning Institute at Temple University) in 2013. The course started with ten or fifteen people in seven sessions. It quickly snowballed into a class limited to forty now offered in thirteen ninety-minute sessions. The course is taught in the fall semester, followed by a spring semester film festival he curates and leads on related topics.

The course informs and illuminates their world for the lucky students who register early enough, and it expresses views that have taken root and matured in Bob's heart and mind starting early in his seventy years. How he reached this point and how he continues to grow are evident in his story: a boy from a modest row house in northeast Philadelphia, educated in his parish parochial school who has come to consider himself "a citizen of the world."

His story echoes so many coming of age stories from the late 1960s and early 1970s. In a time of ferment—Vietnam, Kent State, mounting student voices, and his sociology studies at La Salle University—Bob absorbed changes in his wider world and in himself.

FIRST AWAKENING

One of the things that happened to me in college, which was a big turning point, besides the radicalization of the era, was getting a summer job between my freshman and sophomore years. It was at Ritter Finance Corporation "chasing delinquent accounts." I was living in an almost all-white neighborhood, and that job took me to people's doors in North Philly, South Philly, and West Philly. I'll never forget knocking on my first door at 16th and South. It was really hot; an African American woman opened the door, surprised and not happy to see me, but she invited me in and opened her refrigerator to get me a drink. There was nothing in the fridge but water and milk. She didn't even know about the loan her husband had taken out.

Part of the job was that you were to try to get that person to come with you, on public transit, to the office to pay their loan, or whatever they could. And I actually succeeded in that, which was hard to believe. I met a whole other world of people of all races that I hadn't really met before and just became attuned to situations and physical realities and everything else that I hadn't been conscious of before. The guy who was my supervisor was already a Vietnam War vet. He was a bitter guy.

Among the voices that really spoke to Bob in that tumultuous period was Michael Harrington's. His book *The Other America* and other writings, as well as his founding of the Democratic Socialist Organizing Committee (DSOC) were key influences. Bob attended the founding convention in New York, and when he returned, started the Philadelphia chapter.

With a master's degree in Urban Studies from the University of Wisconsin, and later an MS in Public Health from the University of Massachusetts–Amherst, Bob's professional career usually found him in executive positions in the public health field, directing or leading agencies, finding and solving problems, growing their outreach, and improving services. The role of "the guy in charge" was satisfying when he was able to diversify staff and make services available to new populations.

His work took him with his young family from Massachusetts to Worcester, Ohio, where he directed the Health Management Services' planning for an eight-county mostly rural area for several years. Returning to Philadelphia, Bob took over the Health Promotion Council (HPC), which went from a budget of about $200,000 to over $4 million under his leadership. With an expanded and newly diversified staff, he developed an increasing emphasis on disease prevention and created education programs in chronic health problems such as diabetes, the effects of poor nutrition, high blood pressure, high cholesterol, and asthma. HPC pioneered in "health literacy," creating readable materials about health topics for their constituent population and earned many grants for programs they created to advance public health.

PURPOSEFUL WANDERING

After eighteen years, Bob left the council, feeling burnt out, to take a year off. He then became executive director of the Philadelphia Senior Center, again broadening services successfully. He negotiated the center's absorption by a larger group and found that he would no longer be needed.

Thus, in 2011 began a period of "retirement," which Bob defines as a "constant exercise in creativity."

I was pretty shell-shocked initially, although I had three months' notice and worked for three months after that. My wife is a poet (and professional scientist), and I had begun writing poetry a little bit before that; I started writing poetry about what it was like to be retired. One of my first was called something like "No More 'The Man.'" For twenty-five years of my career, I had been "The Man—in charge. I was used to that, and suddenly I'm just me, sitting in my house. A persistent thought was, "OK, it's Tuesday afternoon at 2:30. My purpose in life is what?"

I volunteered at MANNA (Metropolitan Area Neighborhood Nutrition Alliance), which feeds neighbors in need. I discovered OLLI and took classes, doing some things I hadn't done before: play-reading, improv, and poetry—nothing political. But after a while, I started to think I could probably teach here, realizing I had always been a good speaker in front of groups in my jobs. I was working with the United Nations Association locally. It was part of my ongoing global consciousness thing.

A BURST OF CREATIVITY

Through his UN involvement, Bob learned about the Universal Declaration of Human Rights, spearheaded by Eleanor Roosevelt in 1948.

It provided a coherent focus for Bob's own basic beliefs and hopes for humanity. It became the basis for his course, which includes a wide array of guest speakers and an enthusiastic audience.

I'm sort of the human rights guy in the UN Association now here in Philly. I organize the program every year for the December anniversary of its signing. This year the topic will be health as a human right. My classes occasionally change; last year I added "Muslim Identity in America," for instance. I find that of the hundreds of people I've taught, only two had ever learned about the Universal Declaration before. One of them had gone to a Quaker school.

I have a whole lot of groups I really like and belong to, including Amnesty International, Human Rights Watch, and Human Rights First. The first mission of Human Rights First is to make the United States live up to its values. They do as much as they can to get Republicans and Democrats involved. John McCain was involved with them. My heroes in life now are two types of people: human rights researchers who are on the ground in the worst places in the world documenting these things and getting it out, and then journalists who are involved. One of my classes is on "No free press, no democracy," and I've gotten to know people at the Committee to Protect Journalists in New York City. I've had them down here to talk. This year I added a segment on fake news.

Since the last election, there's been a Trump overlay in comments in some form in just about every class, although not totally. The very words I had spoken the year before about basic rights, which in some cases sound clichéd, suddenly became more meaningful because they were under threat in a way we had never experienced before or anticipated.

Through people who attend the class and its many guest speakers, Bob has been asked to speak on its various topics in other venues. He tries to fulfill as many requests as possible. Bob Groves knows he alone cannot fix the world or change the future, but he can make each step he takes count.

HOW TO CONNECT!

Amnesty International
https://www.amnesty.org/en/
Catholic Charities USA
https://www.catholiccharitiesusa.org/find-help/
Committee to Protect Journalists
https://cpj.org/
DSA Democratic Socialists of America
https://www.dsausa.org/
Harrington, Michael. *The Other America*. New York: Scribner, 1997.
http://www.simonandschuster.com/books/The-Other-America/
Michael-Harrington/9780684826783
Human Rights First
https://www.humanrightsfirst.org/
Human Rights International
http://www.un.org/en/sections/universal-declaration/foundation
-international-human-rights-law/index.html
https://www.ohchr.org/EN/AboutUs/Pages/WhoWeAre.aspx
MANNA (Metropolitan Area Neighborhood Nutrition Alliance)
http://www.mannapa.org/
OLLI (Osher Lifelong Learning Institutes)
http://www.osherfoundation.org/index.php?olli
Philadelphia Senior Center
http://philaseniorcenter.org/
Public Health Management Corporation (PHMC)
http://www.phmc.org/site/affiliates/health-promotion-council
Share Our Strength (SOS)
https://www.shareourstrength.org/
No Kid Hungry (A program of SOS): https://www.charities.org/
charities/share-our-strength-no-kid-hungry
United Nations Association of the United States of America (UN-USA)
http://unausa.org/
UN Universal Declaration of Human Rights
https://www.un.org/en/universal-declaration-human-rights/

· 9 ·

Kendall Hale

POWER TO THE PEOPLE

*K*endall Hale thinks it all started for her in Madison in 1968. That was the year during the anti-Vietnam war turmoil that she began her first two years of college at the University of Wisconsin.

Things started heating up in 1966 and 1967, but it really peaked during those first two years. It was the fall of 1968 when I was eighteen years old that Madison was kind of the epicenter of the whole thing.

On Monday, August 24, 1970, at 3:42 a.m., four Vietnam War protesters, calling themselves the New Year's Gang, had detonated a stolen van containing two thousand pounds of an ammonium nitrate-fuel oil mixture after parking it outside Sterling Hall, the physics building. Their target was the Army Mathematics Research Center (AMRC), which was housed inside the building. A series of articles in the Daily Cardinal *[University of Wisconsin–Madison Newspaper] had claimed that research conducted there was aiding US military efforts in Vietnam.*

The University of Wisconsin–Madison alumni magazine, *On-Wisconsin*, also published a remembrance of the bombing in the Fall 2010 issue.[1]

After that bombing, Kendall left school and formed a women's collective in Portland, Oregon. It lasted for a year. She returned after that year to finish her degree at Madison.

But her activism had evolved from her childhood years with her parents, who were both raised in the Mormon faith in Salt Lake City. It would be a mistake to underestimate the effect of her parents'

51

experiences on Kendall's development, her personality, and her spirit. Although much of their history took place before she was born in 1950, it had everything to do with the choices they made raising her and her two sisters.

My dad never stuck with the Mormon Church even though his mother was deeply religious and totally devoted to the church. He had six siblings. His father died when he was ten, so he struggled. He had to work at a very early age. He just had jobs all the time. They were very poor. My father got out and had to work at the Hotel Utah. He always told me that he began to meet people who came there who were not Mormons. There were blacks, and there were other people. So I think he began to drift away and he left the church.

My mother came from a more middle-class family, and they were not as devoted Mormons as my father's family. My mother's mother was a teacher. When she married, she was pressured to give up her job and stay home having babies. I think my mother's mother was a very talented woman. She was very much aware of how much she was discriminated against; she wasn't very happy. She felt unfulfilled. That influenced my mom. I think that by the time my mom was ready to graduate from high school, she had made up her mind that she didn't want to be a member of the Mormon Church either. So my parents shared a similar position.

Her parents were "very patriotic." With the outbreak of World War II, her father joined the navy and her mother joined the WAVES.[2]

My mother's first husband had been shot down over Italy. When they came back from the war, they both went back to the University of Utah. My mother didn't complete a degree, but she read enormously. The New York Times *and the* Nation *were read in the house. She kept seeking and learning. I think they were engaged citizens just because that's what their youth demanded of them.*

With the passage of the GI Bill (Servicemen's Readjustment Act of 1944), her father had the opportunity to study at Columbia University. The family moved to Shanks Village in Rockland County, New York, into a very meager former Army barracks that had been converted into housing. Veterans going to college in New York City were given priority in occupancy. They had "very strong moral values."

Now they had close friends who were young, Jewish, African American, and had also come out of the war, just a lot of different types of people living there close together. They were finally being exposed to the world's diversity. And there were so many interesting professors at Columbia during that era.

It just really shaped their view of reality quite profoundly compared to how they grew up.

Ultimately, Kendall's father became a political science professor at Ohio State who would discuss philosophy and different philosophers with her that he had trained under or read when he was at Columbia.

So I think my parents really identified with people who were less fortunate than they were and with oppressed people.

After completion of his studies at Columbia, the family relocated to Columbus, Ohio, where her mother became a civil rights activist. Soon she persuaded Kendall's father to follow suit. In 1963 they marched in Washington to protest the war in Vietnam. Her parents were righteous and upstanding role models for her activism.

My mother was very creative, and I share that, although not to the same degree. She was also an early feminist. In Columbus, she joined the Unitarian Universalists. My father stayed away from joining any religion for his whole life. I was raised with my father being an agnostic/atheist, and my mother taking me to church. I was aware of the Unitarians by the time I was in high school. I guess I had gone there as part of their youth programs.

And I really do seek out spirituality. But just so you don't frame my childhood as this idyllic thing, that's the one thing I think was sad for my parents. They never mentioned anything to do with the afterlife or with a god or a great spirit or a force. There was nothing ever spoken about Jesus or Buddha. We never even came close. Once my mother stopped going to the UU, I had to seek my own sources. And I am very spiritual. I definitely have always had a bent on wanting to know where we came from and where we're going.

HER ODYSSEY

After the war in Vietnam ended, with her college degree in hand, Kendall hitchhiked to New York City and eventually wound up in Cambridge, Massachusetts. There, in 1973, she studied at the Cambridge-Goddard Graduate School for Social Change, an alternative graduate institution established to study left-wing politics. During her time in Boston, Kendall worked for three years in electronics plants. Ever the activist, she tried to organize a labor union with her coworkers, who were primarily women. In those three years, she had become a full-time revolutionary and had been fired from four plants that she described as "sweatshops."

Kendall had always played the violin, and as she labored for social justice, music was a balm for her soul. At Cambridge-Goddard, she heard a women's group singing, and she connected with them.

You know it just was amazing because everything seemed to overlap in those days. You could get involved in so many different aspects of social justice. And then, of course, I was in this feminist band that we created right after I moved to Boston in 1973. We named ourselves The New Harmony Sisterhood. The women's movement was just huge. We were like a family. So we were out there singing and raising money. We wrote a lot of our own music, and we were very popular. We were invited to perform to raise money for many different groups. We did that for about seven years in the Boston area. So there just wasn't anything you couldn't get involved with. It was a sign of the times, certainly. I was sure we were going to build a third party, a Labor Party.

The New Harmony Sisterhood performed until 1980, singing their commitment to the issues of the 1970s such as feminist goals, protesting nuclear power plants, and their link to the Boston women's movement. When they disbanded in 1979, they had a solid record of performances and recordings. In 2006, Smithsonian Folkways reissued the band's 1977 single, "And Ain't I A Woman?"

At the same time, 1976 was the year for Kendall to learn to weld. She worked as a welder for two years at the General Dynamics shipyard in Quincy where she was one of only fifty women among five thousand men. Affirmative action had made her hiring possible. The women worked on liquid natural gas tankers under dangerous and unhealthy conditions.

Kendall was very class conscious. She demonstrated for civil justice issues and heard a great deal about the views of Lenin, Marx, Mao, and Che Guevara. Her father gave her many of the volumes these men had written. She wanted to see the truth for herself and to continue her "seeking." She traveled to China, Peru, Nicaragua, and Cuba to hear the revolutionary leaders speak and to talk to the people being affected by their teachings, sometimes living among them. Everywhere Kendall traveled, she found that things were not as she had been told or as she had imagined from her research.

In Dorchester, Kendall met handsome Steve Norris at a union drive. He had dropped out of West Point and was a union organizer. He was earning a living as a carpenter/handyman. Completely taken with Steve, Kendall moved in with him. They became a couple that went to or led many demonstrations to heighten awareness of social injustices: protesting the Vietnam War, working with Black Panthers, opposing imperialism in Nicaragua, engaging in women's liberation sessions. Robin Morgan's book, *Sisterhood Is Powerful: An Anthology of Writings from the Women's Liberation Movement*,[3] energized her determination to bring justice to the struggles and issues of the time in Dorchester and then in Mission Hill. They built a passive solar house on a forsaken lot at the back of the hill that Steve bought from the city. They were both involved in fighting the city's demolition of low-income housing that stood in the way of hospital expansion, and they could not prevail. Heavy equipment, hospital guards, and local police arrayed against the protesters, who had to retreat. They continued to work for social justice causes, and then an opportunity came to them.

In 1991, a friend of her husband's from Boston days invited them to share a property with him and his partner, so they moved with their young son and daughter to North Carolina. They came to know the incredible wonder of the area, and by 1993 they found a beautiful twenty-acre property of their own in Fairview, near Asheville. Kendall named it Sharon Spring. This is where she plans to spend the second half of her life, in this idyllic space in the Blue Ridge mountains.

EMBRACING PEACE

Together Kendall and Steve landscaped half an acre, established a pond, and planted a sustainable garden.

We weren't farmers, but we were like caretakers of this gorgeous land, and we had done a lot of landscaping, established a pond. We had cattle, we had pigs, and for a while we had goats. We had become very, very engaged in being self-sufficient. We tried everything; we were just wildly enthusiastic. We lived connected to nature.

However, they needed more income than her husband was earning, and Kendall could not find work. Although she did have a job for a while in legal services, she knew that was not what she wanted to do. In Boston, she had been studying meditation, and Asheville was now a place where New Age healing was taking hold. The economy had turned to the service sector and tourism. She went to massage school and established a massage practice. She became a yoga trainer and built on Chinese energy work, which offered hands-on healing, polarity, and Reiki. She found her calling in the Asheville community, which by 2000 had become a tourist mecca with commercial businesses and alternative medicine. Sharon Spring became home for Kendall and her family and a wellness retreat for visitors when she added a rental cabin, yoga and meditation lessons, a sauna, and massage services.

After years of work, she published *Radical Passions: A Memoir of Revolution and Healing* in 2008.[4] Her husband serves as a catalyst, a being who shares her beliefs and encourages her activism.

There were times when I was barely making any money, but our family did OK because my husband always had a salary. That kept me able to explore. And our marriage lasted.

To be sure, Kendall has maintained her activism. Today they are focused on climate change and environmental justice. They continue their commitment at the local, state, and national levels. Their particular issue is the Atlantic Coast Pipeline, which is proposed to run from Virginia through eastern North Carolina.

There was an awakening here in Asheville as things moved on. There were people who had already been reading Bill McKibben. And we had one of the first of 350 environmental organizations here. There are so many back-to-the-landers who were already here, and there've been ecologists and environmentalists too that it just flowed right into the fact that we're burning coal and we had Duke Energy, which was polluting with coal-fired plants here.[5] And then that became a focal point. Then everyone who was interested and had the time or the means to start mobilizing and organizing and spreading information got involved.

Kendall considers North Carolina ideal for wind farms and private solar companies. She is determined to protect the environment for all of her granddaughter's generation. It is an important cause and a paradigm shift that Kendall will work to actualize. In her memoir, she credits her family's values for who she has become.

My conclusion—only when more of us can embrace forgiveness, awareness, kindness, generosity, and selflessness to all living beings will our civilization be prepared to take the next evolutionary step forward to a politics guided by love rather than hatred.[6]

HOW TO CONNECT!

Clean Energy
https://www.energy.gov/science-innovation/clean-energy
Hale, Kendall. *Radical Passions: A Memoir of Revolution and Healing.*
Bloomington, IN: iUniverse, 2008.
Morgan, Robin. *Sisterhood is Powerful*: *An Anthology of Writings from the Women's Liberation Movement.* New York: Vintage, 1970.
TED Talks, Alternative Energy
https://www.ted.com/topics/alternative+energy
350.org
https://350.org/about/
Top 10 Things You Didn't Know About Wind Power, August 23, 2018.
https://www.energy.gov/eere/wind/articles/top-10-things-you-didnt
-know-about-wind-power
Yale Environment 360
https://e360.yale.edu/features/why-bill-mckibben-sees-rays-of-hope
-in-a-grim-climate-picture

IV

SOCIAL MEDIA AND THE NEW SENIOR MOMENT

*W*hat part do social media play in your life? Do you Tweet? Follow people who buttress your opinions? Use FB? Contribute money to causes? To candidates? "Like" a meme, an event, or a piece of news? Count your friends? Find old classmates? Send pictures of your family, your new haircut, your favorite dinner? Use emojis?

How do social media play a part in your life? They may be connectors to a wider world just at a time you feel your own may be shrinking. As physical challenges appear and people you knew are no longer there, they can fill empty spaces, spark new connections and revive old ones, and relieve loneliness or isolation.

Just the act of "liking" something on Facebook or hitting "Follow" on Twitter can evoke a good feeling. Actually engaging in comments or conversations is another step into the social media world. But is it *activism*?

The kind of "feel good" liking of something or sharing a link on Facebook, and then doing nothing further about the cause you liked, has been labeled "slacktivism" in recent research.[1] Showing support for a cause so easily, Kristofferson says, obviates the need to put in the kind of effort that makes for lasting change in behavior.

In another world, using social media can be your *entry level* activism when it leads to more action than liking or linking. It may lead to advocating for a cause in the real world, to getting involved in political campaigning offline, to finding satisfying ways to contribute to the changes you want to see.

Count the new senior moments you experience when you use social media as an activist—not a slacktivist!

TR

Lynn Holbein

FIND YOUR VOICE; SPEAK YOUR TRUTH

*P*eople often wonder what their legacy will be. They wonder how future generations will tell the story of their lives, what the remembrances will be, how well the achievements in their lives will weather the passage of time. But these thoughts are more the province of seniors than the generation of their grandchildren, whose necessary focus is *now* rather than the unseen future. Perhaps the mindset is a product of longevity, of life experience, or of realizing the limits of our mortality. Although these contemplations can be fleeting for some, for others a legacy emerges quite clearly from the pattern of their lives.

In the case of Lynn Holbein, she always knew that she wanted to help people. Growing up near Washington, DC, she was very much aware of national issues. At home, her father was a proud northern liberal while her mother was a ladylike southerner who was horrified by the thought of doing anything controversial. That was not the only contradiction in her early years. She was educated at a private religious school for girls in Arlington, Virginia, where the culture emphasized more than college prep. The girls in that school, as in many similar institutions of the day, were groomed to become respectable wives, to raise proper families, and to join the Junior League.

THE TIMES THEY WERE A-CHANGIN'

Lynn enrolled in Oberlin College, in Ohio, the first American college (in the 1830s) to admit blacks and women as well as white men. For her, in the mid-1960s, there was still a nine o'clock curfew for women with the possibility to add a two-hour sign-out to go to the library. This younger generation was questioning their parents' expressed mores and established standards of conduct.

The campus was invaded by The Pill and recreational drugs like peyote, LSD, hashish, and marijuana. There were Vietnam antiwar upheaval, political assassinations, and the identification of the "generation gap." Everyone had the chance to stand up and be counted. It was easy to romanticize—to "air-brush"—the experiences. But this was one of the scariest, most confusing, and most complicated decades in our lives. Some families were torn apart. By junior year I thought I was majoring in drugs and demonstrations. When we were arrested for civil rights demonstrations, they would drop the charges. I would call home to say that I had been arrested for civil disobedience and my father would say, "Great!" while my mother was shocked.

During those college years, Lynn's parents divorced and suddenly, for her, "all of the personal stuff was mixed up with the societal turmoil." It felt like an extension of the unrest of the time. In 1967 the March on the Pentagon took place.[1] It was the largest anti–Vietnam War protest to date. Lynn was among the estimated 35,000 protestors.

A flame from the Peace Torch in Hiroshima was brought to San Francisco in August, and it was walked across the country to Washington. An empty moving van was loaded with marchers. Small groups of four or five would take turns "grasshoppering," walking the flame about five miles at night. Along the route, people would sleep in churches and join the walk. I caught up with them in Cleveland, and that flame arrived on October 21 on the steps of the Capitol. I got locked up there.

THE BEAT GOES ON

After college, Lynn met her husband. During the first four years of marriage, she worked full-time and couldn't give time to her causes. It was the only time she was not an activist. But after their first child was born, she stopped working. She was breastfeeding when she heard about the Nestlé boycott, which was started in Minneapolis by the Infant Formula Action Coalition (INFACT).[2] The boycott became a campaign that spread from the United States to Canada, Europe, New Zealand, and Australia.

In some underdeveloped countries, Nestlé was accused of aggressively marketing baby formula to women who could not breastfeed or who saw the formula as a safe and alternative way to feed babies. Among the many issues raised was that this was an expensive product.

At first observation, the formula-fed babies seemed to have a higher mortality rate. Mothers were malnourished themselves and often died as well. The World Health Organization (WHO) recommended a total ban on advertising for formula.

However, a study of eleven cultures, many in third world countries but also in American cities such as Houston and Los Angeles, revealed that although the formula is safe under certain conditions, impoverished mothers living in unsanitary conditions often lacked refrigeration and clean water. Others did not understand the directions well enough to mix the formula correctly.[3] These concerns made it impossible to predict that babies could thrive on formula if prepared under these circumstances.

Major manufacturers had found a lucrative income stream. Three American companies dominated the US market, but in the much larger global market, Swiss-based Nestlé had a 50 percent share. Lynn worked on this problem for three years. Eventually, *60 Minutes* entered the conflict. She was interviewed in her home and appeared on the TV program.

In 1984, six and a half years after it started, the Nestlé boycott was resolved. The company agreed to comply with the WHO international code of marketing of breast-milk substitutes.[4]

SWORDS INTO PLOUGHSHARES

For Lynn and her husband, the next few years saw them add two more children to their family. In 1982 and again in 1983, President Ronald Reagan referred to the Soviet Union as the "evil empire" and vowed to increase military spending and to "roll back communist expansion in

Third World countries."[5] The world was suddenly aware of the renewed arms race between the Soviet Union and the United States. When their second child was two months old, Lynn heard Dr. Helen Caldicott speak.[6] She founded the Women's Action for Nuclear Disarmament.

She came to my Unitarian Universalist church and gave her talk as the sermon. Her talk was always the same. She would ask what would happen if a one-megaton nuclear bomb hit the closest big city, which for us was Boston. Then in twenty minutes, she would give a detailed and graphic description of the devastating results. Many people were activated by her shocking and vivid talks.

Then my best friend and I and six other women started a chapter of Newton Action for Nuclear Disarmament, which at one point had 800 members. And then I got involved with a variety of organizations at the national and local level to work on that. That was because I was afraid my children would die in a nuclear war.

For Lynn, that was the beginning of a thirteen-year effort toward nuclear disarmament.

The MX Missile was a nuclear weapon that could obliterate cities because of its powerful structure. When launched, it separated into ten different warheads. The first country to launch could eliminate enemy weapons across the world. Many activists were working to defeat the passage of a congressional bill to fund more of these missiles because it was considered incredibly destabilizing. In the 1980s, in response to this issue, a woman I know said, "I think I know how to stop the missiles." Then she contacted six or eight other women to join the group, which was called The MX Missile Project.

For three years we met in my house every month. We were each assigned a congressional district represented by a possibly "persuadable" congressperson and the constituents in the district. So we each spent our time trying to contact the churches that had peace groups. We contacted all the church groups, all the peace groups, any group that could persuade. We asked them to contact their representative to urge them to vote against the bill to fund the missiles. That was how I met Linda Stout, founder of the Piedmont Peace Project in North Carolina.[7] To fund these weapons, there would have to be cuts to social and healthcare funds. Linda met with representatives, and her whole thing was we need daycare centers, safe water, good schools. We don't need MX missiles.

When the vote was finally taken in 1982, the bill was defeated. The vote was 245 to 176, with 50 Republicans joining 195 Democrats in voting down $988 million to start building the missiles. The overall plan would produce 100 of the new weapons at an estimated cost of $26 billion. It was the first time since World War II that either house of Congress has voted to deny a president funds for the production of a significant weapon.[8]

INSPIRATION

Linda Stout has been a powerful inspiration for Lynn. She is the author of *Bridging the Class Divide*, published in 1996.[9] Besides the Piedmont Peace Project in North Carolina, in 2000 she founded Spirit in Action "to seek out transformative tools, models, and resources for building a powerful and visionary progressive movement."[10] She is one of fourteen sisters and a thirteenth-generation Quaker who would not be stilled.

Despite scholarships that took her to college, she was too poor to afford an increase in tuition. She had to drop out. She learned about racism and classism through her experiences working in a North Carolina textile mill and where she was organizing working people. When she left the mill, she found a job in a civil rights law practice.

So a lot of the time and especially in the 1980s, I tried to figure out how to export the liberal energy outside of Massachusetts to other parts of the country. Then I met Linda in 1985. I figured that I could serve someone who is doing this work. I've known her now for more than thirty years, and I do things (like locating donors) so that she can continue the work. Linda's been in danger from the Ku Klux Klan many times, and at one time she needed funds for armed guards. I found the four wealthiest women I knew, and I hosted a lunch. When they heard her story, these women helped her.

My husband and I gave her some computer equipment, and now that's part of what she uses to teach online in twenty-three countries. She trains activists. She is an activist's activist.

CONCORD MINIMUM SECURITY PRISON

Lynn got involved in volunteering in the Concord minimum security prison because of two of her friends who are also social justice activists. One friend would often encourage her to join the programs of the

Concord Prison Outreach (CPO),[11] an organization that started in Massachusetts in 1968 and works cooperatively with the Massachusetts Department of Corrections.

I was very busy with my activism, and I'm very loyal to my causes. At the time, I was also teaching art to adults, often in church-sponsored settings. However, eventually, another friend, a member of my Unitarian church, went to a meeting where someone stood up and said that Concord was looking for an art teacher. When he came back and told me it got my attention.

Now, I have definite opinions. I think that I have a higher power, which is very much aligned with my conscience. And when I am involved in social justice work or in making the world a better place, I feel that I am aligned with the life purpose that I have been given by this higher power.

And I know that higher powers don't necessarily come to us as thunderstrikes; they come to us as a lot of people giving us messages that we can listen to or ignore. This time I kind of felt that my higher power was sort of tapping me on the shoulder and saying, "This means you. Ignore this at your peril."

Concord is a men's prison, and women can't go in alone. I had to have a partner. I said, "OK," and I recruited a woman who also goes to my church to go with me. She was a former student in my art class. I contacted the prison, and I said we would do an eight-week class. This month is our eighteen-year anniversary. I'm still going every week, and we have three other women who have joined us. That means that we go on average once every other week. We're still going strong after eighteen years.

At first, I taught a watercolor class. But that's cumulative learning and attendance could be irregular at Concord. So I stopped teaching watercolors, and now we basically preside over a two-hour session where the men can draw or paint. But for the most part, they come in to make greeting cards for their friends and family, often for their children. We literally have hundreds of stencils and templates for cards. We play a lot of music, pretty loud, some in Spanish and some in English.

For all my work, it is with UU Mass Action that I knew that I made a decisive difference. I mean literally, all the time I worked on these huge issues. When I got involved in criminal justice reform, specifically, mandatory minimum drug sentence reform, I was intensively active for fifteen years, at least. That was my number one issue until last April when Massachusetts passed a sweeping criminal justice reform bill. That took hundreds and hundreds of volunteers. I had worked on it myself for years, and now I see men in my prison art class who are getting out early because of that bill.

MACRO-MICRO TRANSITION

Before retirement, Lynn worked on social justice issues in a "macro" environment. As a full-time advocate, she chose to tackle major issues with gusto and enormous energy, to use her strengths and her wits where a large population would benefit.

She served on the board of the Partakers' primary program, College Behind Bars.[12] She founded UU Mass Action, a state-wide social justice organization whose mission is to organize and mobilize Unitarian Universalists in Massachusetts to confront oppression. "This is my greatest accomplishment." She served as president for eleven years.

There is now a Lynn Holbein award that reads as follows:

> UU Mass Action created this award in honor of our founder and board president, Lynn Holbein. Lynn founded UU Mass Action in 2005 and was our board president from 2005 to 2017. She continues to serve as UU Mass Action's vice president. It was through Lynn's vision for a more unified UU social justice movement in Massachusetts and her dedication to transforming a dream into a reality that our UU State Action Network came into being.[13]

Moving into her seventies, Lynn continues being an activist extraordinaire, with her focus primarily on fewer far-ranging activities.

When I turned seventy, I quit Mass Action, leaving it in incredibly capable hands, and I left the board of the College Behind Bars program. I continue teaching and being cochair of my social action committee.

Now I'm about to start organizing for my thirty-eighth Walk for Hunger, three weeks from tomorrow. I have to collect pledges. My first year to go on this walk was thirty-nine years ago, when I was pregnant with my middle child. In the past, I started out collecting eight hundred dollars. I go to all my neighbors and my preacher. Now for the past few years, I've raised five thousand dollars a year.

I still teach in prison. I was just there last night, and I'm going tomorrow for all-weekend workshops on alternatives to violence in prisons. This whole time I've been a Unitarian Universalist, and I've been the chair or cochair of the social justice committee at my church, which has about twenty-five projects that are ongoing. Now my projects are small or medium.

CARE CALENDARS

Lynn is also deeply involved in care calendars.

If you were doing it for me, you would go online to www.carecalendar. com *and follow the directions. Then you would talk to me. And you would say to me, "I know you're going in for surgery next Friday or I know you just had a baby. Tell me what kind of help you need." I might tell you that I would love meals three times a week and visits on the two alternate weekdays. Then you would go online and create a calendar like that. You make an e-mail list of everybody at our church and everybody in our neighborhood and any others I suggest that you e-mail.*

Then you e-mail all those people, and you'd say, "As you know Lynn will have surgery next Tuesday. She's asked for some meals and some visits." Volunteers sign up online to help out. After the initial organization of perhaps two or three hours, you would never have to lift another finger again. The volunteers receive reminders a few days before the day they volunteered to do something. When you come to deliver a meal, if I don't answer the door, I might be taking a nap. But there's a cooler on the front step for you to leave what you have brought. Most of the calendars are divided between six and eight weeks of care with volunteers for almost every single day.

BEDROCK PRINCIPLE

The guiding principle of Lynn's life is the Serenity Prayer: God, grant me the serenity to accept the things I cannot change, courage to change the things I can, and the wisdom to know the difference.[14]

You mentioned the Serenity Prayer. Has that been an influence in your life?

Absolutely, absolutely. In fact, I would say that I live by the serenity prayer. And it informs me in many ways.

Basically it enables me to unclutter my mind because I say to myself, "Is doing this going to cause me to alter my actions?" I'll give you an example: if I listen to the news or read the newspaper, I know that I'm going to be very emotionally dragged down by them. I ask, "Is that likely to actually do anything to change the situation?"

Three months before the last election, I said to myself, "What can I do?" And I figured out what I could do and then I did it, and I avoided all that emotional clutter. This is totally following the Serenity Prayer.

Lynn is troubled by the current political situation. But last September she put out the word that she was going to do paintings of homes and pets on commission to support candidates she believed in.

I raised two thousand dollars, and I found an organization that was matching contributions to candidates they thought would have a really good chance of winning. Not a really good chance, a fifty-fifty chance. They were all the way from Texas to New Mexico. And it felt good just to raise a little more money that could make a difference. So I donated to that group, and all but two of those candidates won.

Have you ever wondered what one person can do to effect change? Perhaps, like charity, it must begin at home with outreach, courage, and commitment.

> Never doubt that a small group of thoughtful, committed citizens can change the world. Indeed, it is the only thing that ever has.
>
> —Margaret Mead (1901–1978)

DAILY PRACTICE

Every morning Lynn starts her day with a personal practice. She meditates. She examines her goals, which can be big or small: health, family, friends, art, making the world a better place, and the steps she takes toward those goals. They used to always be big steps; now they are smaller. Then she prays and counts her blessings.

HOW TO CONNECT!

Helen Caldicott, M.D.
https://www.helencaldicott.com/about/
Concord Prison Outreach
https://www.concordprisonoutreach.org/
The International Baby Food Action Network (IBFAN)
https://www.ibfan.org/
Massachusetts Peace Action
https://masspeaceaction.org/
Nadwornly, Elissa. *Getting a College Education, Behind Bars*
https://www.npr.org/sections/ed/2018/12/06/592860649/prisoncomics
Partakers: College Behind Bars
http://partakers.org/college-behind-bars/
Spirit in Action
https://spiritinaction.net/about-us/who-we-are/linda-stout/
Unitarian Universalists Association
https://www.uua.org/
UUMass Action
https://www.uumassaction.org/
WAND
https://www.wand.org/about-us

Lynne Iser

ROOTS

*L*ynne Iser, sixty-nine, grew up in a warm Jewish family in Brooklyn with parents who were involved in the community—community meaning a group in which members matter to each other and to the group. In fact, community building was a core value that informs all of Lynne's activism. Her parents clearly lived their ideals. They worked to further social structures that contribute to a better world. Right was a significant teaching in their home. It became a strong foundation for her to build on.

Her father was an elder in their Brooklyn synagogue, and her mother was a committed member of Hadassah. Lynne remembers an incident when she was a child. She attended a meeting with her mother. During that meeting, her mother rose to speak. At the time, Lynne was "so embarrassed" by the act that drew attention to her mother that she wished she could hide. Now she looks back on the principled model her mother provided as an illustration of social responsibility.

I'm glad one of my memories of my childhood is seeing my mother stand up in a meeting and speak out about what she believed. At the time, I was just horribly embarrassed by the whole process. But, you know, she felt strongly about her values.

Hers was a family that practiced "charity." Not charity in the vernacular sense but in the Talmudic sense: Tzedakah, meaning righteousness, fairness, and justice.[1] There was always a Tzedakah box in their home to collect coins for those in need. As one of the Three Pillars of

Existence in Jewish law and tradition, Tzedakah is described as acts of loving-kindness. Thus it follows that Lynne would go through her life as a leader doing acts of kindness and making the world better.

Lynne believes that her generation of "Baby Boomers" has the responsibility to use their resources to "fix" the world and to speak the truth for "the welfare of all, including future generations." For her, that is the essence of elder activism. She describes her activism as bringing her a "multitude of blessings. The more I have become engaged and outspoken, the more I have received."

Yet Lynne did not consider herself an activist until about ten years ago. Her daughter was reading the newspaper and was anguished by the "mess" the world was in.

It seemed to me that if I wanted to leave her, and all of our children, a world that is sustainable and just I needed to become engaged as an activist. And that grew out of a greater critique, a look at what was happening in our world. It's not just civil rights or the war or the need for better healthcare. We really do have to take care of the world.

Now she says she is a "full-time" activist. But perhaps she has always been an activist with no need for the label. Her recent activism took her to Washington, DC for the Women's March and to Standing Rock, North Dakota in 2017 and to McAllen, Texas in 2018. But her preference is to work on local matters. Lynne has lived in many parts of the United States. Each locale has benefited from her contribution.

PATHWAYS

Immediately after her college days at Cornell, Lynne moved to Eureka, California in rural Humboldt County, where she worked to improve nutrition among the poor and increase "the availability of freestanding birthing centers, midwifery services, and home births." In the mid-1970s, she earned a master's degree in public health from the University of Texas–Houston, where she "started with nonprofit organizations, community services, and did a community nutrition program." Returning to northern California in 1984, Lynne helped to establish one of the first homeless shelter programs in the area. She worked there in public health for eighteen years.

INSPIRATION AND INFLUENCE

Always eager to study and learn, Lynne was moved by the writings and workshops of Rabbi Zalman Schachter-Shalomi (known as *Reb Zalman*), father of the Jewish Renewal movement.[2] She moved from California to Denver in 1990 to study and to work with him. Together, they examined what it means to grow older. The result was the creation of the nondenominational Spiritual Eldering Institute, an organization that affirmed the importance of the elder years. Reb Zalman believed that elders have more in common with each other than just sharing the same religion or culture, so a nondenominational approach was ideal. Indeed, it was he who originated the concept of Sage-ing®.

Spiritual Eldering is the process of becoming an elder; of reviewing one's life; of coming to terms with mortality; of finding one's personal truth and the meaning of one's life; of effecting intergenerational healing; of transmitting one's wisdom learned through life experience; of creating one's legacy; and of being a mentor to others.[3]

With the philosophy and mission of the institute established, Lynne moved to Philadelphia. She knew how to design and set up the structure of an organization: things like how decisions are made, strategic planning, rules by which an organization operates, distribution of work, and fund-raising. She became the founder and first executive director of the nondenominational Spiritual Eldering Institute.

Before these people retired after working very hard, they looked forward to a time of comfort in retirement, maybe doing the things they had not done earlier. Yet that way of thinking was changing. That perspective was appropriate for the 1950s and 1960s. But by the 1980s and 1990s, we were having a much longer lifespan, and people didn't want to just retire to enjoy playing golf or painting or playing bridge or whatever there was for relaxation or recreation. They were older people who were then called seniors. It was a time to receive senior benefits.

We defined what it is to become an elder rather than just growing old: "an elder is a person who deserves respect and honor and whose work it is to synthesize wisdom from long-life experience and formulate this into a legacy for future generations."[4] *We now call it Sage-ing® instead of aging.*

But where were the role models? Many of them had passed. The Spiritual Eldering Institute could fill that need.

Lynne's leadership style invites people to participate. "Credit" and personal recognition are not her goals. When the institute was fully developed and relocated to Boulder, Colorado in 1998, Lynne could leave the institute with a capable staff that she had trained and a sustainable infrastructure in place. Today the institute has evolved to be Sage-ing® International.[5]

And then I realized that I needed to focus on the responsibilities of being an elder. This was not a time when you could wait for your neighbors to do something. I was also hoping to inspire young people still in school to take the bull by the horns and speak up.

My initial activism took the form of studying, teaching, and organizing. I started teaching Pachamama Alliance workshops and organizing a local Pachamama community.

Pachamama is a word that comes from the indigenous people of the Andes. Its meaning is what we might refer to as Mother Earth. They understand it to be not only the earth itself but the whole network of relationships on earth. It is the energy that flows among people, from us to the earth and other animals and so it's that. It's almost God-like energy. It's earth-centered and people-centered.

The vision that informs the Pachamama Alliance's work is of a world that works for everyone: an "environmentally sustainable, spiritually fulfilling, socially just human presence on this planet—a New Dream for humanity."[6]

One of the most effective ways to produce results is to empower other organizations through skillful alliances. Amazing things can be accomplished when people aren't worrying about who's getting credit.[7]

FULL STEAM AHEAD!

Seeing the multitude of problems we have as a society, Lynne wanted to know what could be done to work out these perils. Her quest brought her to Joanna Macy, PhD, who said, "Of all the dangers we face, from climate chaos to nuclear war, none is so great as the deadening of our response."[8]

Early on in my exploration, I discovered the work of Joanna Macy and used her paradigm to understand what is happening in our world. I now use her teachings in synergy with the Sage-ing® work and to inspire others to connect with their love of this world, their fears and despair, and to use these feelings to fuel their sacred activism.

Joanna Macy has created a groundbreaking framework for personal and social change, as well as a powerful workshop methodology for its application. In the face of overwhelming social and ecological crises, this work helps people transform despair and apathy into constructive, collaborative action. Her wide-ranging work addresses psychological and spiritual issues of the nuclear age, the cultivation of ecological awareness, and the fruitful resonance between Buddhist thought and postmodern science.[9]

She is a scholar of Buddhism, general systems theory, and deep ecology. Lynne was profoundly affected by this eco-philosopher and her book *The Work That Reconnects*.[10] The Work is described as that which heals the world, and her books have been translated into many languages. This Work is also known as Active Hope,[11] "which is something we *do* not something we *possess*." Dr. Macy's teaching guides activists to tackle ecological challenges and social issues at their source. Since Lynne is a person who often initiates, this mantra was especially instructive.

Lynne's husband, Rabbi Mordechai Liebling, is a lifetime activist who was trained by Joanna Macy in The Work That Reconnects. He is the founder and director of the Social Justice Organizing Program at the Reconstructionist Rabbinical College.

We teach workshops that incorporate both Pachamama and Joanna Macy's principles. Our workshops can be found at synagogues, churches, community centers, and libraries, and we have organized a group that meets here in our home monthly. I call it the Be the Change Circle. This is a study–action group of eleven people. The group came from my sense that I knew a lot of "stuff" and I was learning a lot, but I wasn't really doing as much as I wished. I wanted to plan how to really respond to the issues of fossil fuels or uses of energy or a sense of place or building community organizations.

INTENTIONAL ACTION

Now on a crisp November afternoon under a colorless sky, Lynne Iser and I sit in her cozy living room talking about her intentional commitment to work locally for climate change and social justice. This is intentional because Lynne has made the informed choice to use her energy and resources to mobilize people in her communities. She is dedicated to helping people decide how they want to go forth in this time of their lives.

In my career as an "elder activist" I recognize that not only do we need to reclaim our role as elders but we must reclaim our "voice" as Elders—whether that is at our dining room table, out in front of City Hall, at a community meeting, in a letter to the editor—or a letter to our children. And to speak what is true for the welfare of all.

Besides the Be the Change Circle, Lynne coordinates and facilitates a monthly Pachamama Gathering and a Positive Aging Lunch Series to inform and share the actions and experience of local elders. She created Elder Activists[12] to inspire, educate, and organize elders to work toward a thriving and more just world. Lynne also serves as a Sage-ing® International mentor. More recently she has gathered concerned elders into the New Jim Crow Study-Action Group to study the mass incarceration of African Americans as a contemporary form of racial control.[13]

When someone is this involved, you might think that she would be frantic. Quite the contrary, Lynne is calm, resolved, compelling. She is a leader, an organizer, and a facilitator who knows how to work in a team and how to delegate. She doesn't have to be the center of attention because the focus is always on the principle and the cause.

There are some issues that we all can agree on, and we need to reinforce each other. It's important to speak up, to show that we care. And that's a lot of the reason why I do what I do. I want to encourage people, especially elders, to stand up and speak about the values that they hold.

Some of us might call our life experience wisdom, and sometimes wisdom seems like a big word. But we do have wisdom. We do have a long-term perspective. We have a sense of what is really right and what's important. Like integrity. Yes, it's important to talk about integrity.

As I have studied issues, marched, and lobbied, I have been surrounded by other elders who share my concerns. We feel a sense of unity and strength as we work together to leave our legacy for our children and grandchildren. I believe the Boomer generation could truly make a difference if we reconnected with the values that animated our activism in the 1960s and revived our long-ago ambitions to improve civil rights, safeguard the environment, and work for peace.

Imagine if a return to activism inspired even a fraction of the 10,000 "Baby Boomers" who will turn sixty-five today and every day for the next nineteen years! What a better world that would be. We could be the ones to push our world toward a tipping point.[14]

Lynne Iser uses every day to choose opportunities to live her values and to speak what is true for the welfare of all. Her example is an inescapable challenge to all of us to perform acts of loving-kindness that have an abiding and positive outcome in the service of a better world.

HOW TO CONNECT!

Angry Tias & Abuelas of the Rio Grande Valley
   https://www.facebook.com/angrytiasandabuelas/
Conscious Elders Network
   https://movetoamend.org/conscious-elders-network
Elder-Activists
   http://www.elder-activists.org
Granny Peace Brigade
   http://grannypeacebrigade.org/
Pachamama Alliance, "Mission & Vision"
   https://www.pachamama.org/about/mission
Pachamama Alliance, "Game Changer Intensive Online Course"
   https://www.pachamama.org/engage/intensive
Poor People's Campaign, "A National Call for Moral Revival"
   https://www.poorpeoplescampaign.org/
Praying with Lior (film)
   https://www.imdb.com/title/tt1164092/
Sage-ing International
   https://www.sage-ing.org/
"Zalman Schachter-Shalomi, Jewish Pioneer, Dies at 89." *New York Times*, July 09, 2014.
   https://www.nytimes.com/2014/07/09/us/zalman-schachter-shalomi-jewish-pioneer-dies-at-89.html

V

SKIN IN THE GAME

"Skin in the game" is an expression that's been on my mind lately. It's often used currently in the context of decision making, and its origins can be traced and mused on by language lovers who Google the phrase to their amusement, edification, and ultimate satisfaction. I'm thinking of it in relation to activism, however.

Having "skin in the game" means the difference between thinking, worrying, talking, and agonizing about something and acting. The "skin" in this case stands for your whole self. It involves physical as well as mental activity, whether through writing, marching, cooking, yelling— you name it—that makes you actually feel your emotion physically. In the doing you can sense a whoosh as anger leaves your body and turns into a feeling of strength. It's as though a balloon has been punctured and frustration is subsiding. Relief!

The feeling is good. The skin is in. What is the "game?" The game is the cause. The game is the thing you worry about, whether it's the planet, the plight of children separated from their parents, the disease that is impacting the life of a loved one or yourself, nuclear proliferation, illiteracy—again, you name it. It's the thing that keeps you up at night or invades the sleep that finally comes.

For some people, the game is their profession, their art, or their family. And that is enough. For others, however, something else becomes a very real focus of concern, another game, a cause, something in the world that must be fixed.

TR

Dana Kelley

Non nobis solum noti summus. (*Not for ourselves alone are
we born.*)

—Cicero

*C*icero said it in Latin, of course. He said it, as he did for millions of
others, for Dana Kelley, who has learned and grown through her openness to the suffering of others. Still learning, still growing, still marching, still helping. More, at eighty, than ever.

A SENSE OF POWER NOW

Dana Kelley, of Narberth, Pennsylvania, is convinced that seniors are
not yet aware of their power. She had an indication of the potential
when she was arrested during the Washington march, after marching in
Selma and in North Carolina, a few years ago:

*When we got arrested, the police were terrified something would hap-
pen to us. I mean, can you imagine Facebook and Twitter users if one of their
grandmothers got hurt? Because the police were saying, "Would you like a
chair?" "Would you like some water?" And they wouldn't put handcuffs on us
because we might lose our balance and fall. I thought, "Ooh, man, we could
really go places with this. We could be such a moral voice!" I'd be willing to
put myself on the front line and get hurt. Just being around other good people
[on the marches] and knowing you're on the right side feels really good. I feel
that bad things happen when good people do nothing.*

FAMILY TRAUMA

Dana did not grow up feeling powerful. In fact, the security of life in Marietta, Ohio in a family of teachers was shattered by a health scare few people born after the early 1950s remember. Dana, born in 1940, remembers that frightening time well for the impact it had on her own family.

People born later may remember that polio, a terrible disease that had no cure, struck and crippled thousands of healthy, active children without warning. President Franklin D. Roosevelt founded the National Foundation for Infantile Paralysis in 1938, with its "March of Dimes" fund-raising effort started to help people care for their polio-stricken family members and sponsor research for a vaccine. Dr. Jonas Salk announced the first effective vaccine in 1953, following the report of 58,000 cases the previous year. Dana's family was among the many affected. Her older brother and sister both contracted polio.

MR. STERLING

Dana's brother recovered; her sister, five years older than Dana, was paralyzed from the waist down and wheelchair-bound for life. Their Methodist church community in Marietta, Ohio was there to support them. One man in particular has always remained an important figure in Dana's life.

When my family was going through this, a man named James Sterling kind of adopted our family during this time. He was sort of like the town poet. I think he must have noticed that I was being a bit neglected, which was understandable. (My mother said, "Dana, you're a wonderful child," and I got that I had to be perfect. Couldn't bring any more challenges to this family!)

Mr. Sterling sent a little card to my hamster. And if he'd call on the phone, he'd say, "Oh, I'm so glad I got you, and I hope the sun is shining in your heart today." He always seemed interested in what I thought about things. I remember he said, "He's dead, yet does he live. What do you think that means?" Then they had a big surprise party for him after church once down in Wesley Hall. It must have been his eightieth birthday. And he took me by the hand into one of the rooms on the side. And he said, "You know, Dana, I'm not afraid of dying. I've had a wonderful life. But I'm going to miss something. And that's seeing you as a grown woman." My son's middle name is Sterling.

AFTERMATH

I had an aunt who was a social worker, the head of family service in Cleveland. Because of what she was seeing, she changed to medical social work to prepare people's homes for when their kids were coming home with polio. She was able to get my sister to Warm Springs.[1] I went down to visit her a couple of times there. In fact, I revisited the place a few years ago and went through the exhibits. There was a picture of my sister, doing a weaving project. An iron lung was exhibited. My sister was very smart, always a straight-A student. She married her high school sweetheart, who became a minister. When he got his ministerial degree at Oberlin, she got her master's degree at the same time. They had three children. They had a wonderful family. Then in 1969, the family was driving to Cleveland for Friendly Town, a program that took kids out of the ghettos to stay on Ohio farms. My sister was driving with hand controls. It was a Friday afternoon. Suddenly, a motor mount failure caused the steering and brakes to fail; the car started going over an embankment and hit a tree.

Dana's brother-in-law was killed. Her sister had twelve broken bones. Her two-year-old was in a coma for a month and brain-damaged. Dana flew home.

My sister was in one hospital, my niece in another. My mother said, "Don't upset her. Don't upset her when you go in there." I walked in and just started to bawl. And we both just cried and cried. My sister said, "Doesn't everyone else care?" I told her they were trying to be strong.

Having been through social work school and the grief, and seeing so much, we became peers. She was always my big sister, but we became peers, and were extremely close ever since. I got to see her die and be there [some forty years later].

NEW YORK

Dana arrived, prepared with her degree in English and Sociology, to live in New York with three sorority sisters from Miami University of Ohio. Her first job was as a social worker at the Brooklyn Aftercare Clinic, for mental patients (as they were called in those days) who had been released from the hospital and had to see a psychiatrist for medication.

That first job was amazing. I had seen very few African Americans, never a Puerto Rican in Ohio. Never met any psychiatrists. I saw every kind

of schizophrenia except catatonia. And the psychiatrist I reported to had been
a student of Freud's. He was in his seventies, and if I would go to ask him
a question, he would pull me in the room and give me a kiss. Another looked
like Rasputin and had been head of the Romanian youth group during the
war. Another was a Jungian. One day, a black woman came in, and she said,
"You're going to be my social worker? What do you know about life?"

"Nothing," I said.

If patients didn't come in, I was supposed to go and find them. Years
later, I thought that if my daughter had wanted to do this, I would never let
her. But I never was accosted or had anything bad happen to me. Dr. Rieger
(my supervisor) was fascinated by my background. He said, "You know, when
you grow up slowly, you can grow up well. You were lucky." For some reason
I had enough background, I thought, and I always knew, "I'd better get out
of here now."

Within two years, I realized that [credentialed] social workers were
earning double what I was, so I went back to NYU for my master's degree in
social work.

Dana's eyes were opened very wide through the lens of New York
life and through life as a social worker there.

When I was going through the situation with my sister, my supervisor
asked how I was. I started telling her about my sister, and she said, "No, how
are YOU?" and I cried and cried, and she just sat there. That was one of the
biggest gifts.

And Dr. L., the head of the Jewish agency where I worked, was a genius
who worked on the codes during WWII. He would ask about my sister and
advise me on whom to call about her and about my niece, and what to say
to the doctors. I got how much he cared, and I loved working there. One day,
I was talking about bias and growing up, and I flipped my bagel over, and
Dr. L. said, "You can't just come to New York and think you can just eat a
bagel like that!" But then I came in one day and said, "Oh, my god, I really
got Jewed." And there was silence. I had never seen that written. I mean I
just grew up with that.

BECOMING A UNITARIAN

Dana married at thirty. Her husband George's career as an attorney
presented an opportunity in Philadelphia. The change was hard ("no
tall buildings!") until she started working for Family Services. Then

their daughter was born and, when she was three, asked, "Who's the Lord, Mommy?"

I thought about her education. I went to the Quakers first and found it too somber. I read about Unitarians in the newspaper and investigated. I found there was nothing I'd have to let go of, or say "Oh, I don't believe that!" George, whose mother was Jewish, didn't have a problem with it. So that's how I became a Unitarian. There are times I'm jealous of the focus in Judaism on education and philanthropy.

Years of social work, parenting, a divorce after twenty years, and a long-term relationship were all times of challenge and continuing personal growth.

BECOMING AN ACTIVIST

Dana credits her participation in the Landmark Program with having been a key factor in her personal growth and development.

Becoming an activist was actually through Landmark. They have different programs you can do. The first one is a Landmark Forum; then there's the advanced course. Next, there's a program called Self-Expression and Leadership. You're supposed to take what you learn and take it out into the community and do a volunteer project of some kind—not to benefit Landmark, but to expand your tools. You come up with an idea, enroll other people in your program, and then you give it away—over a period of six months. You would be amazed by the programs that started this way.

Through church, I met and worked with Mahin Bina, a Jewish woman from Iran, who created the End Violence program at Graterford Prison. I never felt like I was really "enough" yet to start a program myself, but I realize that I thought I couldn't really hurt people in prison. Whatever I would give them would be something, at least.

MAIN LINE UNITARIAN CHURCH

The Main Line Unitarian Church, in Devon, Pennsylvania is led by Reverend Dr. Neal R. Jones. The church has six very active outreach committees: Criminal Justice Reform, Reproductive Justice, Environmental Justice, Gun Control, Good Government, and Economic

Justice. A representative in the state capital of Harrisburg keeps track of all relevant legislation and lets members know when to act through the state-wide "UUPlan" described on its website. "UU" refers to the Unitarian-Universalist Association of Churches.

Today, Dana concentrates her activism through work primarily on criminal justice reform and with and for those who are presently incarcerated and those who are leaving or have recently left incarceration. She continues to educate herself on successfully interacting with diverse populations.[2]

I'm working specifically with one man who's in prison now and others who are coming out. I'm on the Anti-Mass Incarceration Committee at church. Once a month I call in, and it's on Zoom, and people from other Unitarian churches around the state share what we're doing so we can learn from each other. We're doing expungement clinics, coordinating with other organizations like the ACLU, and trying to do as much activism as we can and educate people.

I care about climate and women's rights. I have many black friends who have worked with me over the years, and I've become very close with some families. And whenever they want me somewhere, I go.

HOW TO CONNECT!

American Civil Liberties Union
   https://www.aclu.org
Change.org—The World's Platform for Change
   https://change.org
The Coalition to Abolish Death by Incarceration
   https://decarceratepa.info/CADBI
Eastern State Penitentiary
   https://easternstate.org
End Violence Project
   https://www.endviolenceproject.org
Landmark Worldwide
   https://www.landmarkworldwide.com
Main Line Unitarian Church
   https://mluc.org
March of Dimes
   https://www.marchofdimes.org
UUPLAN: Home
   https://www.uuplan.org

Gilbert Kliman, MD

$\mathscr{D}$r. Kliman spends more than half of his time in treatment and research, and less than half in litigation that involves traumatized children and adolescents. He is able to reach the many venues in which he is active, including courts around the country, the US-Mexico border, and the Tulalip Native American Reservation in Washington, because he still flies to them, piloting his own plane, as he has done for decades. His dreams of flying and leaping Superman leaps across empty lots when he was a boy have been more than realized, to the benefit of children who need help around the world. Perhaps the experience of thousands of hours of piloting time has contributed to his ease in adapting to so many new technologies, such as videoconferencing, throughout his long and illustrious career.

Born in 1929, he is a Distinguished Life Fellow and Diplomate of the American Psychiatric Association; a Senior Life Fellow and Diplomate of the American Academy of Child and Adolescent Psychiatry; and a Certified Psychoanalyst for Children, Adolescents, and Adults of the American Psychoanalytic Association.

He is currently full-time medical director of the Children's Psychological Health Center, including the Children's Psychological Trauma Center and Cornerstone Therapeutic School Services, all of which he founded. We met in his office in San Francisco. He spoke with great clarity and with humor.

ABOUT TO SLOW DOWN?

I have slowed down a bit—working strictly seven days a week, no more nights!

When I reached eighty-eight, I thought that it might be a good idea for me to anticipate that I was not immortal. Although I kept trying to get an immortality certificate, nobody would sign it or provide it with any kind of authenticity.

So I was going to close the agency I regard really as my youngest child, the Children's Psychological Health Center. I thought I really should begin the closure of it while I'm still cognitively capable of closing it in an orderly fashion, and perhaps transmitting and transferring its knowledge base and activities for others. We actually have passed a motion at our board of directors meeting to do that. But then the US government did something extraordinarily cruel to children and parents.

SLOWING DOWN WILL HAVE TO WAIT

It [the government] started to deliberately deter asylum seekers by separating parents and children at the southern border, a policy the attorney general publicly announced that was intended to deter other asylum seekers. The president supported that policy for quite a few weeks, but at the time the policy was announced, the American Pediatric Association, the American Psychological Association, the American Psychoanalytical Association, and the American Child and Adolescent Psychoanalysis Association had all written position statements foreseeing and warning about the danger of separating children from their parents in a deliberate, abrupt, unprepared way. So I was very alarmed, and I thought that this may be one of the categorical trauma experiences that could be prevented and might be interfered with. And I had so much experience in the justice system that I thought I should bring that skill to bear.

At the moment that I reached that understanding, I was in Chicago, where I was "arm candy" and the "first man" for the president of the American Psychoanalytic Association, who is my wife [Dr. Harriet Wolfe]. I realized that while all these thousands of psychoanalysts were assembled at the meeting in Chicago, I might have an opportunity to shame them into participating in helping the world by stopping this national policy through expert witnessing. It would be appropriate to do so in various cases of asylum-seeking parents and children. So I went about the meeting saying, "Let's stop sitting behind the couch when a nation is in such a moral and social crisis. Let's volunteer to evaluate parents and children at the border or wherever they are if they've been forcibly separated," and 110 people volunteered immediately.

WHAT TO DO . . .

I had over sixty years of experience in courtrooms, giving testimony for a thousand or more people in major and socially influential cases, and I realized that these volunteers had no idea what to do in courtrooms, so I shared my forensic expertise and techniques with online training seminars. Services began, going first to Yolo County, California, where there were some asylum-seeking adolescents who had been very wrongfully locked up in facilities that had no capacity to provide for their needs as traumatized adolescents. Then we went to Dilley, Texas and evaluated mothers and daughters who are locked up, often for many months; detained as if they required San Quentin, with locked doors after locked doors. We weren't able to get in there with our video cameras or audio recorders because the facility was not meeting the need for professional transparency and collaboration. We made a note of that, and now we have met some of those persons who were released into the community and have videotapes of their eye-witness accounts of the cruelties to which they've been subjected.

IMMIGRATION: AN EXPERT
(AND ELDER) SPEAKS

When Dr. Kliman presents research, videotapes, and interpretations of his evidence before judges and representatives of national and international organizations, he is an expert witness in both the legal and literal senses of the term. His accounts are received with great respect, he noted, because they are presented by:

A senior, let's call him an elder, psychoanalyst who's very senior in his field, listening with psychoanalytic ears.

Accounts of observations at the border give voice and documentation of the facial and bodily expressions of victims of emotional cruelty, showing that the principles of the United Nations in avoiding the emotional torture of refugees are being violated at the request of the administration of this country. It appears that the policy includes inflicting enough pain that others will be deterred from seeking the experience [of entering the United States].

We think that the initial adjuring to be cruel has gotten down from the top to the levels of guards, ICE officials, and even psychologists and caregivers in facilities like Karnes, Texas and Dilley, Texas, so-called residential treatment facilities, so-called residential centers. These centers, by the way, are not licensed by the state of Texas but are rather a strange, monstrous creation of the political process.

This work has led to Dr. Kliman's participation as the principal psychological damage expert in a case against the US government and GEO corporation on behalf of thirteen asylum-seeking children and their (separated) thirteen asylum-seeking fathers. The complaint was filed at his recommendation.

MEANWHILE ...

I work with a Native American tribe quite a bit, and one reason that I'm able to do that is I introduce myself as an elder who, being eighty-nine now, is entitled to that nomenclature. And I introduce myself also as familiar with the trans-generational threats of genocides and massacres, and their consequences in all races, roots, and categories of people, just as Native Americans are all too familiar with the consequences. The tribe I've been working with for about four years now is the Tulalip at their reservation in Washington.

Dr. Kliman's work there has brought to a halt and has prevented further plans for special needs Native American preschoolers from being sent away to off-reservation white public schools, repeating the trauma of earlier years when children were sent away to white-run boarding schools and deprived of language and connections to their culture. They now live and stay full-time on the reservation, learning their native language, music, dance, and culture with people trained to carry out his proven-effective classroom method.

He has given, and recorded for distribution, a sixteen-week online seminar series on "Psychological Trauma Seen Through a Psychoanalytic Forensic Lens."

He is working on the case of dozens of boys raped at a residential facility, and children sexually abused in foster care.

Children who have suffered from traumas continue to benefit from the use of a manual Dr. Kliman created, *The Personal Life History Book*. The method for its use and the manual itself have been adapted in Mandarin as a response to the Sichuan earthquake; in Creole, in response to the Haitian earthquake; and to reduce PTSD symptoms among New Orleans schoolchildren displaced by Hurricanes Rita and Katrina.

A treatment developed and practiced at the Children's Psychological Health Center, called Reflective Network Therapy (RNT), has spread far beyond the San Francisco home base to many independent schools and school districts in the United States and in South America. More than forty years of outcome data and changed lives attest to its power in healing "hearts and minds" of children suffering from autism spectrum disorders, developmental disorders, and serious emotional disturbances. The treatment is a social network therapy that enlists and trains those closest to the children, including family members, teachers, and therapists in the treatment process.

Dr. Kliman's current work, told here only in part, has two principal streams. It centers still in direct work with children in need of help because of psychological problems; work on behalf of traumatized and abused children and youth; and, more recently, the legal system effects of evaluations for separated families. Along with this direct, therapeutic, and often forensic work is his concentration on documenting and developing the means of transmitting the knowledge he has as a part of educating and training professionals who do now, and will in future, build upon it to the welfare of countless others. This is work that will go on and be further developed by those who come after him.

THOUGHTS ON AGING

Ours was an extraordinary opportunity to probe such an exemplar of what can surely be thought of as his successful aging about the topic of aging itself. Happily, he is not above sharing the occasional aging/memory-loss joke, but mostly the conversation was serious and unforgettable. He clearly embraces the terms "old," "senior," and "elder" so many ageists avoid.

I think one of the factors contributing to my generativity is that I have almost died a number of times [major medical problems], and each time I remember feeling that, well, it was OK, but I had a lot more to do. It was, I think, a useful experience to have nearly died.

About the work at the border:

As an old, senior, elder civil rights activist whose work goes back to being chased by the Ku Klux Klan in Cincinnati, Ohio, to forming fellowship councils, to integrating a Greyhound bus before Rosa Parks ever thought of the idea, it's natural for me to use my remaining energies and cognitive abilities that I so cherish this way. I'm so grateful for the opportunity to live this long and exercise my skills this long, and apparently to do so successfully. It's a great privilege, I feel.

In response to a question about the work of the psychologist and psychoanalyst Erik Erikson, whose theory described stages of human psychosocial development:

Erikson wrote of a cycle of later life called generativity. I believe that there is a good deal of pruning of the brain that occurs over the course of a life that permits generativity to emerge, [also] creativity and, in some ways, more abstract thinking, less concrete thinking. There is less concern about the practical moment-to-moment thinking and more long-range thinking.

It seemed to me that seniors express a triumph of life over death. During my life, I have lost a grandson and a son, very prematurely, and it appears to me that my reaction is exemplary, and that is, I felt there was a danger that I would allow these dreadful, sorrowful losses to obstruct my creativity. And I determined successfully to increase my creativity, in a sense, to have more grandchildren, and more children of an intellectual and social nature. I think that is what Erikson is talking about, that there comes a time when it's not appropriate to make a child, but it's appropriate to have a child of a more abstract form, which is going to be carrying its children into the future as well.

I think of the evolutionary process as having favored longevity in our species, that it is not necessary for procreation to have elder people. It's not necessary for construction or hunting or agrarian purposes. But having elder people seems to me to be an evolutionary advantage for our species for the preservation of the culture, the information, the experience, the wisdom, the abstract concepts, and the transmission of these by relatively unselfish people who are at stages of life where they are not acquisitive.

HOW TO CONNECT!

Because Dr. Kliman's work has been highly recognized and celebrated, much can be found about his many research articles and publications on the internet. Here is a place to start:

The Children's Psychological Health Center in San Francisco, CA
www.childrenspsychological.org

Selected Books

Kliman, G. *Psychological Emergencies of Childhood*. New York: Grune & Stratton, 1968.
————. *Reflective Network Therapy in the Preschool Classroom*. Lanham, MD: University Press of America, 2011.
Kliman, G., and A. Rosenfeld. *Responsible Parenthood*. New York: Holt, Rinehart, & Winston, 1980.

Jean Lythcott

I am a Pollyanna optimist; my optimism fuels my energy.

I am a science educator. When I am in a science classroom, it doesn't matter whether they are five-year-olds or PhD candidates; I am a fish in water.

I was afraid when I retired [at seventy-five, from Stanford University], what would I do? How would I not yearn for and spend my life longing for what I didn't do?

I know that my work is primarily with young people in schools. I know that world.

I think the notion of intergenerational living and working is crucial.

When I got an A in the Chem course that was said to "separate the men from the boys," the professor on my PhD dissertation committee said, in a public space, "You must have been sleeping with the professor." I said, "Well, thank you very much, doctor. You are no longer on my dissertation committee."

If every eligible person in Santa Clara County, California, including high school students and the unhoused, is not registered to vote and informed about the importance of voting, it won't be because Jean didn't try to reach them.

MEET DR. JEAN LYTHCOTT

The above excerpts from our meetings and interviews with her provide a small window into the life and worldview of Jean Lythcott, a life that began eighty years ago in a village in the north of England. It was the kind of place many of us can imagine: a local dialect was spoken, along with English. Among the thousand villagers, there were three churches: Church of England, Wesleyan Methodist, and Primitive Methodist chapel. Three fish and chip shops. Quiet, nurturing, isolated. Perhaps questioning began when Jean, the teenage assistant organist at the chapel, heard the visiting preacher (no resident vicar presided) lambasting Catholics from the pulpit.

The very first person I had ever met who was different from me was a girl who was a Catholic. And it just struck me as completely at odds with what the chapel had been trying to teach me.

AFRICA AND THE NEW WORLD

In the decades-long journey from that village in England to Palo Alto, the signal stop and start was in West Africa, where young Jean, armed with university honors in botany and chemistry, two years of teaching experience, and a sense of adventure, started anew. In Lagos, Nigeria, she met and married Dr. George Lythcott, a distinguished African American pediatrician who, following his research in the area, was directing a US assistance program as a regional director, helping nineteen countries to combat smallpox and measles. Their daughter, Julie, was born there. Jean's introduction to life in the United States began in 1968 in New York, where George, in his newly appointed position as a dean at the medical school of Columbia University, moved his family. For his white English wife and biracial daughter, a happy family life and cultural adjustments for his wife and child followed. Discrimination felt from many colleagues in Africa who disapproved of interracial marriages had already prepared Jean to dismiss barriers to her own development and self-confidence that were based in gender or racial prejudice.

Work and further education for Jean followed her husband's professional and geographical track, from New York to Atlanta, from Washington, DC to Wisconsin, and to their final years together in Massachusetts after he had been diagnosed with cancer and retired. Along the way, she earned her PhD, was a professor at Columbia University, worked with Peace Corps volunteers in the South Pacific, Nepal, and Swaziland, and cofounded the Martha's Vineyard Charter School. All this before teaching days at Stanford and preparing new students to teach the sciences, and being, as always, a professor who considers teaching "doing something together with" rather than "delivering instruction to."

AN INTERGENERATIONAL, LIBERATED, ACTIVIST'S LIFE

Jean lives in a charming bungalow attached to the larger house, which is home to her daughter, acclaimed author Julie Lythcott-Haims,[1] her son-in-law, and their two college-age children.

My daughter and son-in-law were Stanford students. They both decided that they wanted to come back to this part of the world [after law school in New England]. As an interracial couple, they had never faced the kind of trouble I had. My husband had died. So, they asked if I could come and join them when they began their family. I am fully incorporated in their lives. I think the notion of intergenerational living and working is crucial.

That was borne out in her work with the League of Women Voters (LWV):

When I joined the LWV of Palo Alto, I saw that many of the members had been members forever and were my age. And so in 2016 two things happened: we got two people working on membership, and we had the election. Now, all of a sudden, we're the second or third largest league in the state of California, with all of these new people, these younger women. It's grand!

When I ask what brought people into the League, often they will say, "I had to do something [about the country's direction]."

I find this a liberating time for women, and for men, too. The general expectation was that men are this way, and women are that way, and everyone sort of bought into that.

We welcome men in the League. We have one who's been on the board as treasurer and another who's running our online communication, The Voter's Edge. *They understand that we keep the name "The League of Women Voters" because of its historical significance. It was founded almost one hundred years ago, when women got the right to vote.*

A NEW GOAL FOR THE PALO ALTO LWV

In the time-honored tradition of great teaching, as Jean gained access to all the public and private high school senior students in Palo Alto, usually fifteen minutes to present already prepared registration forms for the students to sign, she and her cohort found opportunities to do more than was first anticipated. A journalism class offered more time, and another teacher said, "Take whatever time you think is important." One asked, "Do you touch on the Voting Rights Act of 1965 at all, because that's on the Advanced Placement exam?"

And I said, "I'd be so happy to touch on that!" And with her, and with the students, I could ask, "Do you know, in the Constitution, when African American men were given the right to vote?" 1870. "When do you think they actually got a chance to vote? Not until 1965." The teenagers were alive and well in this discussion. I was able to tell them the story of why that was how it was—that every little organization would raise a barrier to having men of color come to vote. There was no law that governed the whole thing, so any little municipality might have a legal fight, and so with the county, and on and on and on. Then someone raised his hand and said, "So that's still the case, right?" And I said, "I am so glad you asked that question, because in 2016 there was a lawsuit settled by the Supreme Court." And I could tell them about the case and its repercussions.

So now we have new elections for the school superintendent for the state of California. We are going to write [to that office] immediately to say that in this day and age it makes no sense that teenagers in high school have no sense of history. No wonder they don't vote. Now the superintendent of San Mateo County sent an edict all over the district saying that all the social studies teachers have to take a day with all their classes and do voter registration with them.

We're trying to place ourselves as the activists in schools. We need to get teachers, students, student government, a club in school, which is "Kids for Politics," and "Kids for Registration."

We're meeting now with the publisher of El Observador, *the Spanish-language newspaper published in San Jose, to plan how to best reach all language groups in Santa Clara County and inform them of the coming changes [2020] in how we vote according to the new California Voter's Choice Act. People will have improved opportunities and extended time for voting through this act.*

NOT JUST POLLYANNA

Jean takes heart in the participation and leadership rising among teenagers. She speaks with great admiration of the Parkland, Florida student survivors:

You know, their teacher is credited with enabling them to make clear and succinct arguments and to do public speaking. They marched in the streets in one state after another, and they stayed in the streets until they were heard. And they are winning—in bits and pieces.

I heard from a friend of mine on Martha's Vineyard that when the shooting happened in Florida, there was a response at the school we had founded there. I had instituted a morning meeting at the school every day when we started, and it continues. A senior stood up, moved by what had happened in Florida, and said, "I want to go to Washington to march with them." And all of a sudden a forest of hands went up, and other people wanted to go, and we're going to need a bus, and so on. And Islanders just chipped in money to get a bus; the local high school joined in, and they ended up with several buses, and kids from Cape Cod high schools went, too. I was so moved by this that I wrote to the Vineyard Gazette *and said I was so proud of them for taking this stance. And I said that as you move forward in activism, what I want to do is to challenge them to think bigger. This is about more than background checks and bump stocks. For example, maybe one of the things that we need to do is to recognize that these weapons are a problem for public safety. So what we need is, instead of a department of motor vehicles, we need a department of firearms and ammunition where you have to register them with the department.*

Here is clearly what Jean means about teaching being something she does "together with," providing leadership with ideas and action, and hearing and supporting theirs.

In addition to her work with the LWV, Jean makes time for the writing group her daughter started and, always, for her family close by and her extended family, and work on the quilts she has started for grandchildren. Jean says of her determination to work for voter's rights, for fairness, for the values promulgated by our Constitution and to combat its corruption:

I feel an urgency, but I think it's the topic rather than my age.

Life has gifted me. If I could leave a legacy, it would be that life would treat other women the same way.

HOW TO CONNECT!

American Civil Liberties Union
   https://www.aclu.org
California's Voter's Choice Act
   https://voterschoice.org
El Observador (newspaper)
   https://elobservador.com
Gerrymandering:
   https://endgerrymandering.com
   https://www.fairvote.org/redistricting#research_redistrictingoverview
Indivisible
   https://indivisible.org
League of Women Voters
   https://lwv.org
League of Women Voters of Palo Alto
   https://www.lwvpaloalto.org
NAACP
   https://www.naacp.org

VI

PSSST!
LOOK OVER HERE . . .

*O*h, sorry, did I distract you? Were you doing something important? Listening to music? Watching an absorbing TV show? Talking to a friend? Meditating?

Please, excuse me and go right on with what you were doing. Unless . . .

Perhaps you were anxious about being at loose ends. Feeling depressed. Experiencing physical pain.

If "Yes" is the answer to any of the last three, then please welcome the distraction!

"Why should I welcome it?" you ask. Because distraction from anxiety, depression, and physical pain is a very good thing. Science and experience tell us so.[1]

Consciously or unconsciously, we are always making choices on how we focus attention. Is it on work at hand or a pleasant diversion? Is it on the pain or immediate concern that is blocking everything else out? Is it on what we feel we *should* do rather than what we *want* to do?

Finding a cause that provides a space to develop our own interests, contacts, and awareness of our own potential for "world-fixing" leaves less time for focusing on negative aspects of life. Becoming one of the "fixers" can yield results that range from alleviation of anxiety, depression, and awareness of physical pain to making them actually go away.

When aging brings inevitable changes that challenge us physically and emotionally, engaging in efforts to bring positive change is always a "win-win."

TR

· *15* ·

Cirel E. Magen

CURIOSITY STUMPS FEAR

*F*or Cirel Magen, life has been a constant flow of curiosity. She observes, engages, and questions much of what she has lived. She craves diversity because she thrives on it. Cirel has an expansive perspective on life. This is what has worked very well for her.

Listening to other people who were not like me. I mean, I talk about this. My idea of the perfect meal is, more than a buffet, it's a smorgasbord. And my ideal of friendship is that not all my friends are eighty-two-year-old white women living in Center City Philadelphia, Pennsylvania. I mean, I like having young friends and black friends and Asian friends. Life is a smorgasbord if you're lucky. I don't want to eat steak every night.

She describes herself as "perennially nosy." Abiding curiosity has led her to a life of activism and accomplishment.

When my children were young, I was curious about their schooling, of course, and became involved in the public schools.

I'm not really political. Now that doesn't mean I don't have political passions, but I've never, it's funny, the only political thing I ever did is I was a Republican committee person because we lived in a division in Philadelphia that was 95 percent Democratic. And we couldn't have an election unless we had some Republicans. That's my only formal political thing.

I get involved in causes. I march occasionally, very occasionally. But I'm always out there. After the 2016 election, the Women's March was on a Saturday. After that event, I marched when Donald Trump had that retreat here in Philadelphia. People were so interesting, so good-natured. It was quite an amazing experience.

*But then I write letters, I make phone calls, more on causes and a lot
locally: about preservation things, the conditions of sidewalks, but I'm not
formally political, and I'm all over the map. It really depends on the issue. On
my grave, they are going to write, "there is no detour she would not follow."*

AT MY MOTHER'S SIDE

A favorite cause for Cirel is her work with libraries. The commitment is
deeply rooted in her childhood and her family relationships.

*My passion all my life has been libraries. This is a funny memory. My
mother did the family banking. And the bank was at 56th Street. I grew
up in West Philadelphia, and the public library was a block away. So every
Friday morning, before I was old enough to go to school, she and I would go
to the bank, she would withdraw the cash for the week, and then we would
walk a block to the public library.*

*I recently went back to that branch. They are sensational librarians: car-
ing, wonderful, and very involved in the community, the black community.
And it was a wonderful experience for me, and they really made a big fuss.
I mean how many people do they have come in who have a library card they
got at that branch from seventy-five years ago? It was great.*

Until she retired, Cirel had a full professional life. For many years
she was the director of volunteers in several healthcare institutions. This
seems to be a natural fit for a woman accustomed to being part of the
solution when she sees a need. She still found ways to continue being an
activist. She harnessed her considerable energy to meet the responsibilities of her job and to advance the causes that are her passion.

Later in life Cirel became instrumental in the rescue of the Philadelphia City Institute (PCI), a library on famed Rittenhouse Square,
established in 1852 and not part of the city's Free Library System until
1944. Cirel is the only woman to have served as president of PCI. By
changing investment managers, she doubled the endowment of PCI.
The proceeds of these investments are given to the Free Library "to
improve the intellectual lives of youth."

In 1996 Cirel cofounded the Friends of the Library group. This
group raised enough money to renovate the heat and ventilation systems
in the library building and to occupy a temporary home during the process. Today PCI operates as a branch of the Free Library of Philadelphia

while the board of managers owns and maintains the building, which they lease to the city for a dollar a year.

IN SUPPORT OF LOCAL THEATER

She has always welcomed opportunities to make a difference, and Cirel's curiosity usually leads to direct action. A friend introduced her to the Charlotte Cushman Club, which appealed to another passion, theater. She and her husband joined the club with the encouragement of that friend. Cirel knew that the invitation to join meant an unspoken agreement to go on the board and work for the goals of the club. And she found a creative way to bring together her love of libraries and her love of theater.

The Cushman Club originated in 1907 when there was a need for respectable, inexpensive, safe, and convenient lodgings for actresses who came to the city to perform in plays. In time the Philadelphia theater scene changed. It was no longer necessary to have a boarding house, but the Cushman Club recognized the need to help small, nonprofit groups for theater and the performing arts.

The members sold the clubhouse and donated their library collections to schools and organizations. The profit from the property sale added to the club's endowment and the Charlotte Cushman Foundation was born. The foundation encourages regional nonprofit groups to submit grant proposals to promote small theater performances.

The foundation has been a very gratifying experience. We get proposals from neighborhood groups. The hope is that exposure in these communities will generate an interest and appreciation of theater arts.

The foundation contributes a quarter of a million dollars annually to the Free Library of Philadelphia.

We ask that the money be used in ways that help young people. We are now doing some college courses for people who will not normally go to college and doing some college prep to give support to young people who have shown some promise but are wavering. The Free Library does amazing things. They really do.

The urge to be curious has rubbed off on her son too.

We got an e-mail from him one day saying that he was told that Bing-hampton University is working on an online project, a Dictionary of the

Woman Suffrage Movement. *"They are looking for volunteer writers. Why don't you do that." So I wrote away and thought, "yeah, that sounds like fun."*

Now Cirel and two friends are writing about Pennsylvanian Mabel Cronise Jones. Born in 1860, among her publications she wrote a long poem about the Battle of Gettysburg, an unusual topic for women after the Civil War.

Cirel's curiosity is contagious and a catalyst for those who try to keep up with her. She is a self-propulsion engine. She sums up what makes her an activist in a most eloquent thought:

I am a very, very curious person, and although I'm not the world's bravest human being, when I get curious, I keep going. It cuts out the fear of things.

HOW TO CONNECT!

ALA Libraries Transform
   http://www.ala.org/advocacy/libraries-transform-campaign
American Library Association
   http://www.ala.org/
American Libraries magazine
   https://americanlibrariesmagazine.org/blogs/the-scoop/state-of
   -americas-libraries-2018/
Center for the Historical Study of Women and Gender
   Biographical Database of Militant Women Suffragists, 1913–1920
   http://chswg.binghamton.edu/WASM-US/crowdsourcing/NWP
   _description.html
Community Managed Libraries Network
   https://communitylibrariesnetwork.wordpress.com/author/community
      librariesnetwork/
   https://www.hcn.org/articles/a-community-fix-for-rio-arribas-libraries
Charlotte Cushman Foundation
   https://charlottecushmanfoundation.org/
I Love Libraries
   http://www.ilovelibraries.org/
   http://www.ilovelibraries.org/librariestransform/article/because
      -libraries-make-leaders
   http://www.ala.org/advocacy/i-love-libraries

Independent Libraries Association (UK)
  Independent Library Report for England
  https://assets.publishing.service.gov.uk/government/uploads/system/
    uploads/attachment_data/file/388989/Independent_Library
    _Report-_18_December.pdf
Institute of Museum and Library Services
  https://www.usa.gov/federal-agencies/institute-of-museum-and
    -library-services
Interact Theatre Company
  http://www.interacttheatre.org/mission
Little Free Library
  https://littlefreelibrary.org/
Philanthropy Network Greater Philadelphia
  https://philanthropynetwork.org/
Women's Suffrage Movement Use the Rise of Journalism
  http://teachinghistory.org/best-practices/examples-of-historical
    -thinking/25635

Irene Barnes Mehnert

DON'T JUST DO SOMETHING; STAND THERE!

*T*his might well describe how Irene Mehnert lives her life: in her thinking and in her actions. Earning an EdD in Assertive Training for Women at the University of South Dakota in 1974 (the first empirical study of the subject), provides just a hint. She can be counted on to lead, to participate in the work, or to stand and witness. It depends on the need.

From her birth in January 1932 in Great Neck, New York to life today, with her high school sweetheart husband, in Malvern, Pennsylvania and in Maine, Irene makes every minute count and finds opportunity for action or witness in a world and for the humanity she loves and sees in peril. In pursuit of their own educations and professional lives, Irene and Bill traveled to universities in Connecticut, Indiana, New York, and South Dakota before settling at the one in Orono, Maine, and finally, after life in academia, and into other aspects of the educational world, moving to Pennsylvania.

In everything, she presents a model of authenticity, of modesty, of confidence, and of giving. Irene would not tell you any of this unless you asked or needed to know.

SEEING NEED

Within the past several years, Irene and Bill took a long-anticipated trip to India. Irene described consensus advice from friends and acquaintances who had been there:

"Look," they all said, "there's going to be lots of beggars, and if you give to one, you're gonna be swarmed. So don't look at 'em. Look straight ahead and just move on as quickly as you can."

So we were walking along, and my husband had my arm. This young woman comes up, and she holds her baby up—and I know the scheme—but the baby was definitely malnourished. I could see that, and an empty bottle for milk. Bill grabs my arm and says, "Just keep moving." And my eyes met her eyes. I just looked at her and gestured with my eyes, did it a couple of times, and she got the idea. She went around behind me, and I put my hand in my pocket, and I gave her some money. She came around in front of me and then—just left. Bill never knew anything. He wouldn't have approved.

I want my grandchildren, who are wonderful, but all "entitled" because they come from close, educated families, to experience what it's like for people in third world countries, and to have compassion for all humanity. That's when I came up with saying, "Don't look away!"

That is the way Irene has been living her whole caring, activist, always-present and up-for-a-challenge life. As the mother of five (four sons and one daughter) and grandmother of twelve (six girls, six boys), she has taught them all through example long before she coined the phrase, what she believes is most important: "Don't look away!"

LEARN>TEACH>MENTOR<LEARN<TEACH<MENTOR

From her own days as a star athlete in high school, to gym teacher, to student, to counselor, to basketball coach, to consultant or director in corporate and nonprofit worlds, Irene has made every experience one of learning, teaching, mentoring, and reversing the process for and with others, in a constant, always evolving loop. Whenever she describes a signal experience or turning point in her life, she is quick to name and credit mentors and influences along the way. Role models have been to Irene what she is to so many others. She remembers and always kept contact with the professor at SUNY who was later a dean. She and another professor were:

the kind of women who fought their way to the top and would look down and say, "OK, I had to climb the ladder. Now you do it. I want excellence from you, but I am going to get rid of all the stuff that gets in the way. I am going to do everything I can to help you."

THIS DIDN'T HAPPEN BY ACCIDENT

While her husband carved their path in pursuit of his personal and educational goals, Irene followed from place to place, although she had always been a leader in school and in athletics. As they moved, she made or discovered her own way at each of his stops: attaining her own advanced degrees, bearing and raising a family, and finding meaningful employment. Her eyes were open to opportunities and to inspiration from teachers of all kinds, both live and in books. Two books in particular shaped her thinking and her ability to lead, to manage, and to find confidence and satisfaction in all aspects of her life.

Bill heads toward graduate school:

Oh, boy, now we're into Academia, where the name of the game is Degree. I thought, "OK, I can jump these hurdles, but I don't want to do it just to do it. It has to be personally meaningful for me." I had struggled as a kid because I was a tomboy when I was younger. But I was always the leader in everything I did. I didn't want to be a doormat, but I didn't want to be a bitch. I thought, "OK, what's the middle of the road?"

I struggled with how I dealt with people and situations, wondering if I really was or could be in the middle, knowing I don't want to be submissive, but I don't want to be really in your face. What is assertive, *and what does it mean to me? The way I chose to define it was to look for a win–win in every relationship I had. And that said I would be honest and congruent with what I believed in or whom I was representing or who I was. And at the same time, I would make sure I really respected and listened to where that other person was coming from—that I get to understand them, and they get to understand me, and so, I did that. It was a joy, I mean, personally.*

I read a book called Your Perfect Right.[1] *It made me feel OK, that I was really speaking to the issue.*

Another book that has provided a framework for Irene in meeting the challenges and opportunities in living and in interpersonal relations is *The Four Agreements: A Practical Guide to Personal Freedom, a Toltec Wisdom Book.*[2] She follows its precepts (agreements):

First Agreement: Be Impeccable with Your Word
Second Agreement: Don't Take Anything Personally
Third Agreement: Don't Make Assumptions
Fourth Agreement: Always Do Your Best

PHILOSOPHY IN ACTION

The early 1970s were a time of profound change and awakening for women, with the passing of Title IX, a path to equality for women's participation in educational programs or activities receiving federal financial assistance, and the passage in Congress of the Equal Rights Amendment (ERA).

Irene was painfully aware of discrimination against women when her husband had a fellowship to study at the University of Indiana, and Irene, with three children in tow, filled a one-year opening for basketball coach.

Well, we won the State, won the Midwest, and went to national competition. However, we were always in the garden pages of the Indiana papers. So I called one paper and said, "You know, Indiana has a policy of equal access, so we're giving it to the opposing paper because we're going to nationals. Would you like to have the same opportunity?" I said the same to the other paper, and they said, "Of course!" So we finally got out of the garden pages, even if it was to the back pages of sports.

Next, Bill was on the faculty at the University of South Dakota, and she was a graduate student and basketball coach for the girls' team.

We had to practice with balls from the boys' team, which didn't bounce above our knees. I had to drive the university van, which was like an airport limo we had to bang on to get started. We had to rotate seats so the ones in back didn't freeze in the South Dakota winters. We got to the nationals several times.

The director of athletics was terrible. I thought if he says in public what he said to me in private, we might be able to do something to turn the situation around for girls at USD. There was some fervor then about Title IX. At a meeting with an interviewer about the athletic program with students in the dining hall, I put some plants in the audience. The director's temper was rising. I said to the interviewer, "As the basketball coach, based on my observations, I would recommend that every woman student at the university withhold her student activity fee because she is not being [fairly] represented." The director lost his temper (in public) and said some things he shouldn't have, so a group of students and I filed a Class Action Suit under Title IX against the University of South Dakota. I loved the university, and I still do, but I knew that the only way to deal with this kind of discriminatory practice was to talk about money. So they gave the university three years to come into compliance. I had something like seventeen counted discriminative complaints against girls.

Really, I could do it because I knew I didn't have to live there, because our mothers in Great Neck were getting older and we'd be coming back east. I told Bill, "It's a good thing I won't get tarred and feathered and we can just move out of town."

It was on to Maine, where Bill joined the faculty at Orono. Irene taught briefly, then joined the Teacher Corps, eventually becoming the director for the state. It was a time when she would manage a large five-year federal grant and oversee a youth advocacy project:

Always one of my interests, juvenile justice, was part of it. It involved the university, work with town public schools, five group homes, and the only incarceration unit in the state of Maine.

A through-line over the years since its introduction in Congress, the ERA has been a major focus of Irene's activism, taking her to demonstrations in various states and in Washington, DC. She marches, she carries posters, and she is willing to be arrested if necessary, in feminist and racial justice demonstrations.

One thing that I would like to see in my lifetime is passage of the ERA. I'd also like to see a women's history museum go to the last empty spot on the Mall in Washington. I'll be meeting with some women who are trying to do something about that.

ALZHEIMER'S, MORTALITY, LEGACY

My mom died of Alzheimer's; my brother died of Alzheimer's. I donated both of their remains to Johns Hopkins, and when I die, my brain will also go there. I'm also part of the Baltimore Longitudinal Study of Aging at Johns Hopkins. When I heard about these studies, I looked at my grandkids, and my kids, and myself, and thought, "Which one? Whatever I can do to make a difference I will do."

I was working with DuPont in Planning in Wilmington, North Carolina when I got a call that my mother had died and that if I wanted to have the autopsy needed for the study it had to be in a certain time period. They flew me back and suggested I Fed Ex her remains. I said that wouldn't work for me.

A girlfriend assured Irene that she could be arrested for transporting body parts across state lines, but she put that out of her mind as she strapped the box in the back of her car and drove from New York to Maryland and the Alzheimer's Research Unit at Johns Hopkins.

"What's your business?" they asked at the desk. I said, "Specimen for the laboratory." They told me to put it on the shelf over there, and I looked and saw all this stuff on the shelf and thought, "You've got to be kidding me!" And there was a door that said "No Admission. Authorized Personnel Only." I couldn't sit there for two hours watching people come and go and think I don't know who is going pick it up. This is important. So all of a sudden, I picked it up and walked through the No Admits door and someone on the other side said, "Where are you going?"

When Irene finally got up to the unit office and again was told by a receptionist to "put it over there" on a shelf with other specimens, she burst into tears and said, "But this is my mother." The receptionist summoned a researcher who brought Irene into his office.

He explained to me what they were going to do and why. And when it was all over, he asked if he could walk me out. And he said, "I just want to tell you, we do much with specimens [but] we never connect with the family [of the] person that's involved. I have to tell you, this has made a major difference in how I will view this from now on."

Then my brother who had early onset [at sixty-one] died in a small town in Texas. My niece was "born-again," the hospital and the funeral parlor would not do an autopsy, and I called the University of Texas at Austin and told them we were involved with the study and what was happening. They said, "Fine, we'll come down and take care of it," and they did.

People say that my brother was just like my mother, and I am just like my dad. I hope so. But because of firsthand experiences, there's a strong commitment of feeling that we can do something about this. I think if people know or think they can do something, the majority of people will say yes.

Irene's contribution to research on aging is through her participation in the Baltimore Longitudinal Study of Aging, which is also conducted at Johns Hopkins. Starting in 1958 with men only, and adding women in 1978, it is the longest study in the world of normal aging. All participants are in good health when they are accepted. Her participation involves a three-day in-hospital examination every year since she turned eighty (every three years prior to that).

WOMEN TODAY

I think there is a great book to be written about women our age. What I'm finding with my friends is that we're all living to be much, much older. Most of us are or could be economically independent. And most of us still want to go places and do things. A lot of our husbands do not.

I'm hearing "tick-tock," you only have three more years to live if you're looking at averages and you're still in halfway decent shape. I want to do things and go places, like to volunteer for a research project.

I think now I'm saying, "Wait a minute; now it's my turn," and I'll do exactly what I want to do when I want to do it. And that causes problems. The sense of family and loyalty has always meant family was first for me throughout my career. I think women's longevity is going to challenge the marriage institution for life.

HOW TO CONNECT!

Baltimore Longitudinal Study of Aging
   https://www.nia.nih.gov/research/labs/blsa
ERA: A History
   https://www.alicepaul.org/era/
Johns Hopkins Alzheimer's Disease Research Center
   https://www.hopkinsmedicine.org/research/labs/alzheimers-disease
      -research-center
National Organization for Women
   https:/www.now.org
Title IX
   https:/www.ncaa.org/about/resources/inclusion/title-IX-frequently
      -asked-questions

· *17* ·

Glenavie Norton

*B*eneath Glenavie Norton's soft voice and modest demeanor lie strength, determination, and leadership skills still in evidence in her seventies. Like many women of her generation, Glenavie developed her interests and participation in causes in parallel with her professional career and dedication to home and family. Twenty-four hours in a day could rarely have seemed adequate. We were privileged to learn about not only what she is doing in Philadelphia, Pennsylvania now, but why. And while she confessed to feeling awkward about discussing family background information, which she rarely does, there are aspects to her heredity that might lead one to wonder, could some genetic force be evident in Glenavie's activism?

ROOTS

William Lloyd Garrison, the abolitionist, is my great-great-grandfather. We had a portrait of him when I was growing up. It hangs in the National Portrait Gallery now. So I grew up knowing that. (My husband, whose father was an anthropologist, also grew up with a sense of mission and purpose.) My mother's parents were immigrants from Northern Ireland who struggled here; my father's descended from the Mayflower. There is a statue here in Philadelphia of my ancestor Mary Dyre, a Quaker martyr. My older daughter has Dyre as a middle name because whatever one might say about Mary, she was a very determined woman, and I wanted one of my children to carry her name and perhaps her determination. Mary had been thrown out of the

Puritan Commonwealth of Massachusetts in 1656 for preaching Quakerism (she was a follower of Anne Hutchinson) but returned twice from England at her peril. During her third trip back, in 1659, defying the laws against Quakerism and her banishment, she was sent to the gallows.

I was aware of family connections to Garrison, Dyre, and also to Anne Hutchinson growing up. As for Garrison, I went to a family reunion of his descendants on the bicentennial of his birthday. He had five children, all of whom had children, and as many as could be found were invited to a wonderful occasion in Faneuil Hall in Boston. Former governor Duvall and a Civil War scholar spoke. Most moving to me was hearing, at the beginning of the reunion, the woman who headed Boston's African American Museum. She cried because it was so meaningful to her to be with these descendants. That made me cry, too. I spent more time with Garrison then (reading about him) and thought, "Man, I guess I'm glad he wasn't my father!" But I realized he had moral courage; he spoke up when it counted. He did things that other people didn't dare to do. And I thought, really this is a time when other people are not doing that. We're just not doing that, and that feels wrong to me. I've always had a very strong feeling about social injustice and a need to speak up against it.

FEMINISM—A SURGE OF POWER

I had the benefit of a wonderful education as a child. I was president of my class, a prefect. And then when I became a teenager and in my early adult years, all that kind of went by the wayside. But when I was thirty, I felt as if there was sort of this surge of power. I moved to Philadelphia and went to graduate school at Penn. This was in the early seventies; feminism was burgeoning, and Roe v. Wade was passed. I could get involved in a way that I couldn't growing up in Washington with my father in government. Here I was in a city with local stuff I could sort of walk into and say, "Hello, I'm here!"

I became involved with Women Organized Against Rape (WOAR) and went through their training; anti-rape funding was big. I became the board president, and as we were a founding group of Women's Way, I was a representative from WOAR to that organization. I moved to something called Women's Agenda, which was a statewide group, and lobbied the legis-

lature every year. We actually brought pies to the legislature, saying "We want our slice of the pie," which I thought was very clever!

I felt very strongly about feminism. I was sort of in a second wave of active people. My mother, who was a very smart woman, had felt frustrated in her own ambitions. She wanted to go to college to become an English teacher. And my great-aunt and uncle, who raised her, said no. So what she did was to go to nursing school and became a surgical nurse. She was actually very successful at that. Her older and younger sisters also went into nursing, each eventually earning a doctorate. My great-aunt had been a Red Cross nurse in World War I, so she approved of nursing careers. My mother and her sister were both army nurses, so they had that World War II sense of women making a contribution. My mother, who loved nursing, stepped down once she married my father. So, I think there was that sense of: this is not right. My mother should have been able to do what she wanted to do—my aunt carved her own way in that world. She actually went in with the Normandy Invasion and stayed for two years after, working with concentration camp victims in Nancy. My mother flew back from Europe to marry my father.

POLITICAL ACTION

During that time Philadelphia was celebrating the Bicentennial. The mayor was a controversial figure who prompted protest from many, including both my husband and me. (I married a protestor!) I was invited to join the board of Americans for Democratic Action (ADA) of Southeast Pennsylvania, which was struggling at the time. I sent an e-mail to people who had been involved literally asking, "Are we dead?" That galvanized a response; they nominated me for chair and I did not step down from that position until last year. Now there is an active young group at the helm, and I'm very pleased with that.

THE ENVIRONMENT

I feel we're at a really serious turning point environmentally, if nothing else. And if we don't do something it's possibly the end for us as a species, certainly the end for a lot of other species, and the planet may not be habitable. The

*number of people who don't realize this—or who deny it—is truly frighten-
ing. I have two daughters, and I have to do something to ensure that their
lives will not be unbearable. I may not have grandchildren, but I feel this is
something that I can do for the children who are coming along. I can't do it by
myself, but I feel I need to make a contribution. At the very least, I can march
and have done so in Washington, DC.*

Can you trace your awareness of environmental changes?

*My father worked in the federal government with many scientists and
talked about climate change early on. It was called "greenhouse gas effect"
then. So I grew up with an understanding that it could come, but it was still
a surprise when it came with such a vengeance in this century.*

How did you manage a professional career?

*I was a social worker. I learned late that it probably would have been
beneficial for me to have used my non-paid work as an avenue into the field
that I was most interested in, which really was activism.*

Glenavie retired from her professional career in her sixties, loving
the people she worked with, but accepting that dealing with bureaucracy
was stultifying. Lacking the incentive to strive for upward mobility in
the work world, she found that world less challenging than her outside
interests. It had provided the security she had sought, however, and
work that was of value to the community she served.

AFTERTHOUGHTS

Glenavie thought about our interview and sent the following note:

*Many women of my age, who "came of age" when the world was begin-
ning to change for women and were swept up in a tide of feminism, have a
real awareness of the fragility of our gains and how much we have to lose if
those gains disappear. That is surely why many of us are activists now. And
many of us may have been before. I certainly feel an incentive to keep for my
daughters what I have gained.*

What I do now is

- *lobby legislators as a concerned citizen or member of a group—in
  person, on the phone, via e-mail;*
- *canvass at the time of elections;*

- *provide leadership to and participate in activist organizations such as Indivisible and ADA (both at the Southeastern Pennsylvania chapter level and the national level);*
- *participate in demonstrations; and*
- *get others involved in the political process both at the citizen level and, going forward, at the candidate level.*

I love doing it. I feel I am more truly myself now than I was when I was younger.

We cannot ask for much more than to feel more truly ourselves now than when we were younger.

HOW TO CONNECT!

Americans for Democratic Action
   http://www.adaction.org/
Indivisible
   https://indivisible.org/
Women Organized Against Rape
   https://www.woar.org
Women's Way
   https://womensway.org/

VII

BUT WAIT, THERE'S MORE!
(BWTM!)

$\mathcal{N}$ow, there's a catchphrase we've all heard before. It seems to be attached to every infomercial and radio ad that preys on our consciousness, offering so much more to come if we buy the product being touted. Not only will we get the product, but we are promised double and triple its value. By the time the announcer finishes the sentence, we tune out. Just a meaningless, clichéd come-on, we know.

But wait, maybe there really *is* more. Perhaps there is more meaning to the phrase than we thought—if we apply it in other ways, other situations. For example:

- I just finished watching a terrific mystery show on British TV. Loved the characters. BWTM! Turns out it's part of a long series; I can enjoy the whole thing. I love the binge and the popcorn!
- Picked up a book of stories by P. G. Wodehouse that made me laugh fifty years ago; still giggled. BWTM! Ordered a whole slew of his stories, now in the public domain, in used copies, many free on Kindle. Reading something that makes me laugh every day. It tastes better than what I was taking for laughs (medicinally, of course).
- Uh-oh! I had a fall and hurt my back. My doctor prescribed physical therapy. Three times a week for eight weeks helped a lot. BWTM! The physical therapist says I'm one of the 5 percent of his patients who continue to do the exercises a few times a week at home. I'm feeling and moving better than I did before the fall.

- Upset and depressed about injustices in the news, I went to a meeting with a neighbor about yet another local problem. At least it was an evening out. BWTM! I met some interesting people, was moved by the speaker, and decided to volunteer.
- Volunteering got me interested in seeing what effects our work was having on the problem, which made a difference in getting me out of the house and out of my routine. BWTM! The city is actually going to fix the problem, and our efforts helped make that happen. We made a difference. What a great feeling!

You get the point. Sometimes the smallest action leads to unexpected and salutary outcomes. Whatever happens in life, there is always more, even if it feels as though we're stuck. Positive actions seem more likely to make the "more" positive, too. The "more" will always reveal something new to find, to challenge, to lead to discovering our own depths.

TR

· *18* ·

K. Rashid Nuri

FARMING, FEEDING, FUTURE!

$\mathcal{W}$elcome to the world of Rashid Nuri, geographically centered in Atlanta, Georgia, but now expanded to include a universe of concepts and words that are finally on the lips of the general public: *organic, sustainable, local produce; community-growth, urban farming.* At seventy, Rashid's life can appear to be a blueprint for the goal-setter, a guide for determined-to-improve-something, a plan for a young, budding activist. Not surprising, he's going strong into the next phase while never abandoning the work he started with his first garden crop as a high school student in San Diego. Both his work and his memoir will keep his vision ever green.

I'm not a retiree. I'm a seasoned citizen.

GROWING IS THE THEME

I say I care about growing food, community, and people.

Like so many children in military families, Rashid learned resilience early, from his birth in Boston, Massachusetts through fourteen schools before his family settled in San Diego. Growing food, growing community, growing in service to his people and the world were inseparable parts of his life and still are. Even as he attended Harvard back east, Rashid helped to establish the first organic community gardens during school breaks in San Diego. When he graduated with a bachelor's degree in political science, he went on to study for his master's degree in plant and soil science from the University of Massachusetts, the seeds of future work already planted in his mind and soul.

The end of the 1960s was a time of consciousness-raising and ferment in the growth of "community organizing" as a way of life marked by grassroots efforts from protests against war and against discrimination of all kinds to fostering group identity and pride, and from marching for voter's rights to rock and roll. In those heady, challenging times, filled with possibility and new thinking, feeding people whose sources of food were limited was a need to be addressed, whether the limits were based on unwillingness of large stores to open in poor and minority urban neighborhoods, or on poverty, or on limitations yet to be discovered.

Agricultural zoning laws were not quite ready for the idea of farming within urban areas. In contrast, fifty years later, we see community gardens ranging from the block-sized flower patch tended by thirty participating neighbors on my street to multi-acre swathes of vegetables and fruits in some cities across America. The trajectory of Rashid's agricultural career and vision follows a path that has always included *food, community, and people*, and has been marked by work that has enlarged his vision.

GROWING THE KNOWLEDGE AND SKILLS

There is something very spiritual and magical about putting your hands in the dirt. Working in the soil and just being around the activities of food production impacts people: the energy that is produced transfers to everything else they do. People begin to nourish the foundation—the soil of their lives—by planting seeds, nurturing, protecting, harvesting, and sharing. The garden speaks to you like nothing else can.

That feeling was always there for Rashid as he built a career starting just out of school managing 13,000 acres of farmland in Georgia for the Nation of Islam. Cotton, corn, peanuts, soybeans, and greens flourished, along with cows and chickens. What followed was work managing operations in Asia and Africa for Cargill Corporation, the global agribusiness conglomerate. He worked in over thirty-five countries in agriculture and observed local food economies in the countries where he worked. Rashid brought that experience and knowledge to

Washington during the Clinton administration, when he served as the appointed deputy administrator in the US Department of Agriculture and senior advisor in the Department of Commerce.

Everything Rashid learned through observation and practical knowledge came together as he raised his own children and thought about their future and that of others whose futures portend a world of growing food insecurity and preventable health problems. It wasn't only in Asia and Africa, but right here in the richest country in the world, that access to healthy food was (and is) a growing problem. The facts that we spend more on healthcare than other developed countries yet have children and elderly with poorer health are undeniable. Two major factors were obvious to Rashid: growing urbanization and lack of access to healthy fruits and vegetables. Our dissociation from the food we consume is evident in two major and fundamental societal changes: urbanization and food production.

GROWING CITIES AND PEOPLE
TO MEET THE FUTURE

If you want to go fast, go alone. If you want to go far, go together.

—African Proverb

Well prepared by knowledge, experience, and accomplishments, Rashid could not only envision, but was able to design and establish an environment and programs to meet the needs he had identified. He has done that in the metropolitan area of Atlanta, Georgia, creating a nonprofit model for urban areas everywhere. The organization, which he led until stepping down this year as CEO but remaining as its founder and advisor, is the Truly Living Well Center for Natural Urban Agriculture, known familiarly to its broad-ranging community as Truly Living Well.

Truly Living Well was started in 2006 by Rashid with two partners, Eugene Cooke and Ernest Dunkley, with an experimental plot that expanded to three farms within and just outside the city limits of Atlanta. A fourth was added in 2010. The yield of the farms is far beyond the peppers, kohlrabi, tomatoes, carrots, kale, cabbage, collard, herbs, fruits, and flowers that grow in abundance. The yield can be measured most excitingly in human terms.

Let's consider just some of the ways Truly Living Well changes lives:

- It gathers people together across cultural and ethnic lines who all share the need for healthy food.
- It is a dependable year-round source of fresh produce, gathered by consumers ranging from professional chefs to people using food stamps whose purchases are further discounted according to need.
- It grows food using techniques that emulate nature, relying on compost, crop diversity, and natural cycles to replenish the soil and combat pests. They use no petrochemicals used by industrial agriculture at the expense of the vitamins, minerals, and trace elements that create flavor and nutrition.
- It provides extraordinary opportunities for children of all ages to learn the joy and skills that come from learning to plant and grow food, while they work together in camp and out-of-school activities that will contribute to healthier, more fulfilling lives. (Working in and with nature—without electronic devices! The learning encompasses literacy, math, science, and more in a context and atmosphere where all succeed.)
- It offers a fruitful (pun intended!) volunteer program for adults throughout the area. (Five hundred people showed up on the last Martin Luther King Jr. Day!)
- It is a source for community service sentencing by the Atlanta courts.
- It is a source for schools and parents in educating their children.
- It has a Growing Families program that uses urban agriculture as a family intervention tool to create an environment for mother and child to work together in a new and positive way.
- It transforms formerly deserted or unkempt areas into beautiful, economically viable, and valuable property.

Rashid has seen the changes in young people who have found hope and direction when they found school a frustrating place, and friendships flourish when kids of diverse backgrounds share camp experiences that provide safe, positive learning opportunities. He has seen young people find, as he does, what is "spiritual, magical about putting your hands in the dirt."

THE NURI GROUP

The vision continues to expand for this amazing food revolutionary. It seems that he is beginning again as he moves on. His new goal?

To expand equitable access to the tools for success in urban centers through education, funding, partnerships, and appropriate regulations. The Nuri Group is working to solidify the position of urban agriculture and small farms as a profession, an economic engine, and a tool for building powerful communities.

WHAT WE LEARNED

Rashid's work reflects what can happen when knowledge, instinct, and passion converge in the service of a world beyond oneself. He looks at urban spaces, understanding that 70 percent of the world's population will be urban by 2050. He sees urban blight—with acres of undeveloped and trash-filled ground affecting the quality of urban life in so many scarring ways, and he sees consumption of fast foods that is ruining health and well-being. He also sees the potential in good health, an end to childhood obesity, a means to bring people together, vital economic stimulation in jobs, new professional possibilities in new agricultural settings, a more beautiful environment, and deepening awareness of the responsibility we have for stewardship of the earth.

As always in our conversations with Rashid, he returns to the human heart of his enterprise:

There are a lot of virtues and values that you can get from the garden that transfer to family and community life. "Being Present" certainly is one of them. You have to listen to the soil, listen to the plants. If you're present, in the moment, the plants will tell you what they need and when they need it. Experiencing this, learning this, helps with all other relationships.

HOW TO CONNECT!

Detroit Black Community Food Security Network
  https://dbcfsn.org
Habesha, Inc., Community Organization in Atlanta, GA
  https://habeshainc.org/
The Nuri Group
  https://www.thenurigroup.com
SAAFON (Southeastern African American Farmers Organic Network)
  http://saafon.org/
Truly Living Well
  https://www.trulylivingwell.com

Short Films

A Conversation about Dirt and Hope
  https://vimeo.com/32143937
My Presence Matters
  https://vimeo.com/29863170
Rashid Nuri, Urban Grower, Atlanta, Georgia
  https://vimeo.com/102193012
Who Grows Your Food?
  https://vimeo.com/3456568

· *19* ·

Patricia St. Onge

SHE WALKS THE WALK
AND DANCES THE DANCE

A handsome college-student grandson, home for a mid-semester break from back east, opened the wooden gate for me, and soon I am sitting comfortably in a yurt, sipping tea with Patricia St. Onge. The hilly surroundings are not in central Asia, where yurts have been traditionally found so useful by nomads for thousands of years, but in residential Oakland, California, where Patricia lives with her husband, Wilson Riles Jr., who served on Oakland's city council for fourteen years, on a large oasis called *Nafsi ya Jamii* ("The Soul Community" in Swahili), within the city.

The property stretches to include three houses, another yurt, a sweat lodge, and Full Harvest Farm, home to almost half an acre of urban farm crops and animal life. The office of Seven Generations Consulting and Coaching, which Patricia founded, is also here. Seven Generations is so named to honor the generations who have come before, and to be mindful of those yet to come. For nearly twenty years, Seven Generations has worked with public agencies, nonprofits, foundations, and academic and religious institutions as consultants and trainers, providing culturally based support and strategies to improve their effectiveness.

Along with her life and work at *Nafsi*, Patricia teaches courses at the Pacific School of Religion and at Mills College.

COMING ALIVE

"Don't ask what the world needs; ask what makes you come alive and go do that, because the world needs people who have come alive."

When Patricia found this quote in the writings of Howard Thurman,[1] it more than resonated. It confirmed and informed her realization that as people reimagine their own lives and relationship with others and with the land, they awaken to their own abilities to make positive change in the world.

Patricia's reimaginings have led her from a Quebecois community in New Hampshire, where she grew up with her four siblings and more than sixty-five cousins, to this place and this calling. Talking with her is easy; she is both a natural and an experienced communicator, a person who "has come alive." Now in her mid-sixties, she speaks of the three trimesters of her life.

THE FIRST TRIMESTER (LEARNING TO WALK)

I have two lineages. One is French Canadian, and the other is Haudenosaunee, which the French called Iroquois. My paternal grandparents came from the French side in the seventeenth century, and the other side have been here forever. So my roots on this continent are deep.

Growing up in small-town New England, Patricia was unaware of racism, its depth in this country, and the impact it has on families and communities and neighborhoods, until her late teens.

I had grown up Catholic, a zealous social justice–focused Catholic, and then had gone and lived in a commune for a year. When I came back, I ran into a high school friend who said, "Guess what! I'm not gay anymore!" and invited me to dinner at the house where he was living with some friends. They taught what they called "The Divine Principle."

Up to this point, Patricia had never heard of the Unification Church and the Reverend Moon.

The [novel] theology made sense to me in the particular way it explained evil, and I accepted their invitation to go for a weekend workshop. Thus began two years as a teacher and lecturer when I was doing what felt like significant work in West Virginia. When Reverend Moon was to speak

*at Madison Square Garden, I was invited to go. There, I was so surprised
and heartbroken by the levels of sexism and racism I found within the institution, I actually wrote a letter of resignation. Gordon (my boyfriend) left
with me, and we went back to New Hampshire to get married.*

Back in New England with Gordon, who was African American,
racism became more real. Response to Gordon's race was new to Patricia.

*The first wave of awakening for me was when I returned to the Catho-
lic Church to get married. I went with Gordon to the priest I had been close
with, with whom I had traveled around the state doing Teens Encounter
Christ workshops. He told Gordon he would have to convert, which I knew
was not the policy, as well as agree to raise the children Catholic. As we were
leaving, he pulled me back and said, "We raised you better than this." I was
like that's it, the Church is racist, too. But when you're in a pretty homoge-
neous environment you don't see it.*

*My dad was an incredibly accepting person, and loving; he was happy
that I was happy. My mom's only concern was how we might suffer. My
dad was ostracized from the Lions Club because he had a daughter who was
married to a black man, and the responses of the extended family ranged
from horrible, like refusing to shake hands, to warmly embracing. And that's
really been my experience across the board: a spectrum of responses to what's
going on in our lives and in the world. When I was looking for a school for
my kids, the schools in Boston were in turmoil at the time. I thought, "Well,
I had a Catholic education, and I thought it was a good one," so I went to
the neighborhood Catholic school. I went by myself and asked what the racial
makeup of the school was. The nun kind of quietly said, "Oh, don't worry; we
don't have many Negroes." When we moved to Oakland in 1987, the kids
were five, six, nine, and fourteen, and it was the first time we [an interracial
family] were not an issue. It's not that racism doesn't exist here, but it's very
different and has a different kind of intensity than what we were experiencing in New England.*

SECOND TRIMESTER (WALKING THE
WALK AND STARTING THE DANCE)

Patricia knew through her paternal grandmother of her Iroquois lin-
eage on that family's side. When she was fifteen years old, her maternal
grandfather told the family when he was dying that he was Mohawk.

No native community or any cultural expression thereof existed for Patricia, however, until she moved to Oakland and found the Intertribal Friendship House started by the American Friends Service Committee. It had been established to serve the needs of American Indian people relocated to urban areas, like the Bay Area, when they had been displaced from their reservations. It was a place to connect not only with people, but also with a rich culture. At the Intertribal Friendship House, Patricia's grandchildren and she, herself, learned native dances as well as other native cultural expressions and arts.

Professionally, Patricia's work both expressed and shaped her knowledge and beliefs. Having earned a bachelor's degree in human services from Southern New Hampshire University, she worked for Habitat for Humanity in Boston. She established its western affiliate in San Francisco on moving to Oakland and became its Western Regional Director as it grew.

As the Regional Director, I saw the ways that the charity model really fails all of us, because it creates an us-and-them dynamic. In some affiliates, it was very accentuated, and in others it had pretty much disappeared as people began to see themselves as partners, both the people who were building and those buying the house. In some affiliates, the overwhelming majority of the energy went to supporting the volunteers, who were mostly affluent and Christian. In affiliates where the family worked with the staff on design—were at the center of the process—and then volunteers came to help them do the work, there was a very different feeling. Kawaii, a part of my region, was where this was most evident. It was really beautiful to see that if the homeowners didn't show up, nobody worked. Everything about that work said, "This is your project, and we are here to support you."

We started doing lots of trainings, and then I met my current husband, who was the Regional Director for the American Friends Service Committee. So we were a pair of regional directors. I saw that their work also incorporated advocacy. I started graduate work toward my master of divinity degree at Pacific School of Religion, even though I am not a Christian.

You say you are not a Christian. What is your religion?

For indigenous people, spirituality and culture are all lifeways, as we call it, and so it's not a specific religion. My spiritual practice is ceremony; we have a sweat lodge here on the land, and that is part of our practice. Also, I feel like the church, all the religions of the Book, have contributed to many of the problems we have in the world. They have partnered with the state in doing some terrible things. Again, as in all things, there is also a thread of people and perspectives on Christianity that have held true to what Jesus was trying to say when he was here, so I don't dismiss that thread. In fact, I think that Jesus was a very powerful and amazing man, and the people who follow his teaching authentically have a lot to say and a lot to contribute in the world.

Looking back, I see that almost all of my work was teaching, training, policy advocacy, and filling interim leadership positions in organizations where they were in transition. Now I feel my emphasis shifted vis-à-vis the role I play in the world: from "How do we feed them?" to "Why are they hungry?"

THIRD TRIMESTER (LIVING THE LIFE)

That question, "Why are they hungry?" has led Patricia to create a space and a way of living that reaches within and beyond the family she has nurtured, which includes nine grown children and six grandchildren she and her husband share.

We see this place as kind of a lab, where we have retreat space, an education center, ceremony, and a farm. Our vision is that it will continue to be a place where people, organizations, and communities can relate to the land in healing ways. We use solar and wind energy and compost toilets. We welcome anyone who wants to create a just and sustainable world.

I use the medicine wheel as the guiding principles for my life. In the North, according to the wheel, is the energy of resistance, so I have been a part of Idle No More, which is a native-led climate movement started by indigenous people in Canada. I am a part of the Bay Area chapter.

I see the connection. How else can you explain the use of the medicine wheel in your life?

In the East is where we reimagined the world we know as possible, drawing from ancient traditions as well as our current context. In the South is where we repair relationships, because many relationships get broken in the process even of trying to heal the world; attending to those relationships is important. In the West is designing of the structure that allows us to rethink how we use energy, how we use resources, how we live together, all of that.

On a personal level, it's body, mind, heart, and spirit. When you make teams, when you build community, the North is people who are organized around tasks; the East is people who are organized around ideas; the South is people who are organized around relationships; and the West is people who are organized around information.

So you need all of these kinds of people if a community, and by extension, the world is going to heal and thrive.

Absolutely. There are animal symbols as well. If you only have the North, which is Buffalos, people are driving, driving, driving, and there's never someone saying, "Let's have a potluck; let's sit down together; let's share ideas; and let's build institutions." It's energy alone. But if the Eagle in the East says, "I have an idea," and the Buffalo in the North says, "Let's do it," and the Bear in the West says, "Well, let's make sure we have the information we need" and the Deer in the South says, "Let's make sure everybody is on board," you get the whole thing done in a holistic way.

Patricia would surely deny it, but she seems to embody all of these characteristics that enable the generation of ideas, the energy to implement them, the love of learning that grounds them in necessary information and research, and the gift for making others know they are respected and valued. Her first awakening to racism also awakened her resilience and determination to live a life of authenticity. Through writing, speaking, organizing, teaching, good humor, and spiritual practice, she lives her commitment to progressive social change.

We often speak of people who "walk the walk," referring to those who do more than talk about their ideals and beliefs, but actually live them, put them into concrete action. Patricia continues also to "talk the talk" through her teaching, writings, and consultancies. Her impact and influence grow as she so clearly "walks the walk," and brings depth, humor, and grace with her as she also "dances the dance."

HOW TO CONNECT!

Backs Against the Wall: The Howard Thurman Story
   Documentary film by Martin Doblmeier: http://journeyfilms
   .com/batw/

Fluker, Walter Earl, and Catherine Tumber, eds. *A Strange Freedom: The Best of Howard Thurman on Religious Experience and Public Life.* Boston: Beacon, 1998.

Idle No More
   www.idlenomore.com

Intertribal Friendship House
   https://www.ifhurbanrez.org

The Medicine Wheel and the Four Directions
   https://www.nlm.nih.gov/nativevoices/exhibition/healing-ways/
      medicine-ways/medicine-wheel.html

Nafsi Ya Jamii
   nafisyajamii@weebly.com

1000 Grandmothers for Future Generations
   https://www.1000grandmothers.com

Seven Generations Consulting and Coaching: (510) 530-2448

Smith, Luther E. Jr. *Howard Thurman: Essential Writings.* Maryknoll, NY: Orbis, 2006.

St. Onge, Patricia (lead author). *Embracing Cultural Competency: A Roadmap for Nonprofit Capacity Builders.* St. Paul, MN: Fieldstone Alliance, 2009.

VIII

BUBBLE, BUBBLE, TOIL AND TROUBLE . . .

The chant of those three witches in Macbeth could be interpreted as giving us fair warning: bubbles spell trouble! Not the pretty ones floating from a grandchild's bubble pipe, not the lush ones embroidering a warm, comforting bath, but the bubbles we retreat to when we suffer losses as we age. Loss is a part of living no one escapes.

We are human and healthy when we grieve, and grief accompanies most losses. It always does for those we love, but we also grieve for accustomed ways of living, for faded friendships, for work we enjoyed, and for real and even perceived loss of our own physical strengths and faculties. Danger comes when grief subsides enough for living to resume, with room for adjustment to the new reality, but we've become accustomed to the comfort of retreat, a bubble that feels protective. A bubble may look fragile and easily pierced, but it can become a wall increasingly difficult to penetrate; moving out of it takes strength and courage, even when we know it's the right thing to do.

Great attention has been paid to expected risk factors for early mortality, such as smoking, environmental factors, diet, and lack of exercise. However, recent research has been factoring in the influence of social connection on physical and emotional well-being, and on longevity.[1] It seems that spending time with other humans, even if some may be annoying at times, is really good for us, and isolation is detrimental to our health.

Always remembering that solitude in meaningful doses can be a positive experience and being alone is not the same as being lonely, the message here is that when you engage with others to save the world, your own health reaps benefits as the bubble of isolation bursts.

TR

Catherine Scherer

NOT ALL THOSE WHO WANDER ARE LOST[1]

Cathy Scherer grew up in the Kansas City, Missouri region of the American Midwest. She never ventured out of that geographic locale, even for vacations. She didn't expect to become an internationalist.

I grew up in an extremely traditional, rigid, middle-class family in the Midwest. It was a very insular, closed-minded society, and people in my family also had that mindset.

In the 1960s she attended Drury University in Springfield, Missouri, and then moved to Colorado to teach school. She and her two roommates had summers off, so that summer they decided to spend three months in Europe for an adventure in traveling. That was it! She came home captivated by the possibility of a new type of life, a life that included many diverse destinations and opportunities to explore new-found cultures with the people who lived there. When she returned, she decided to go back to Europe

as soon as possible, for as long as possible. The only thing I could think about after that trip was how to get hired and go back.

Back in Colorado, time passed, and Cathy continued her teaching career. She married a career Air Force officer, and they lived in many places. She stopped working and settled into the life of an officer's wife and mother of two. Eventually, a military assignment took them to Germany. Cathy had not worked for many years, but while in Germany she returned to professional life.

I worked for an international school and a community college that were contracted by the Department of Defense, which provided educational services for military members and their families. I was the regional director for a section of military bases and posts in what was then West Germany.

During that time she and her husband divorced. Cathy stayed in Europe with her son and daughter for ten years, during the mid-1970s through the mid-1980s. As a result, her children both love to travel and explore.

Her parents were getting older, and Cathy believed that it was an appropriate time to come back. Returning to the United States, she settled in Phoenix, Arizona. Reentry to the States required an adjustment that Cathy did not expect. She had to change careers because there was no position comparable to what she had done in Europe. But she also recognized that her decade in Europe had

changed my worldview and broadened my outlook. One of my first "aha" moments was realizing that part of my sense of dislocation [returning to the United States] was that I could not find the center of my community as I had come to experience in Europe. There you always knew where the center was because that's where life happens to you. They had markets there. They had events there. They had festivals there.

I was in Phoenix, in a very large urban area that was spread out all over, so I never knew where the center was. I wondered, "Where does life happen?" I had lived a much more frugal and Spartan life in Europe. And there was all this stuff that you had in the States that was "required" for life here. I didn't understand why you would need to shop at midnight. When I was in Europe, I didn't miss the dishwasher or the clothes dryer. I spent a lot of time trying to reject all of it when I returned.

How did you reconcile and adjust to these differences?

Well, for most of it I just got used to it, which is kind of what you do.

It turned out that the Arizona heat was too much for her. She moved back to Colorado and became a client with a career management firm. Before long, they hired her to do management outplacement for people who were dislocated by circumstance. They might have been fired or downsized, or they might have experienced other reversals. Some had been international executives coming back to the United States who were having difficulty adjusting. As she worked with these clients, she realized that she had struggled with many of the same issues they were facing. There were valuable personal lessons and necessary adaptations that she had made, and she used them to help her clients.

CREATING GLOBAL CITIZENS

As I began to work with these people, I realized that they were going through what I went through when I came back. The question was, "Where do I belong?" I saw that a lot of companies were global. Executives were going abroad and moving into a totally foreign business and social environment. But when they came back, their transition was unsuccessful.

While she was in Europe and when she returned, Cathy had found that she is comfortable as a citizen of the world. Not only was this a valuable asset to an employer who sends an executive to a foreign assignment, but it would be a major factor in helping others to find their comfort level. Reaching this equanimity also produced better international understanding among community members. That was how Cathy became an international specialist.

Her essential challenge was to clarify for companies and for individuals the significance and the value of the innate skills a person brings to an assignment, as well as the skills learned in a different culture. She knew that all expatriates have similar orientation challenges.

Your self-esteem can take a bit of a beating both going out and returning. You are going to be hit with a lot of cultural differences, many of which you can't see or identify: language, art, music, and architecture. You will also learn how gender is viewed, the concept of time, and communication styles.

Of course, these are only a few of the many variables encountered when crossing cultural lines. Different communication styles, body language, touching, gestures, interruptions, all behaviors have different meanings in different cultures.[2]

But each situation requires sensitivity, awareness, adaptation, and resilience. In an unfamiliar culture, coping with differences in everyday life and in professional experiences can be exceptionally demanding when *your personal connections and influence have changed with your location. Internationalism can't be taught, but it can be learned.*

THE INTERNATIONALIST: PROFESSION FOR A NEW CENTURY

Cathy worked doing career counseling and writing articles, manuals, and guides. She designed training curricula and career management programs that would help to identify successful responses to common problems facing expatriates. She was also in demand as a speaker for professional audiences, both domestic and international.

Ultimately, Cathy realized that she had something to say about company globalization and working internationally. She intended to provide an account of what it was like for an individual and a company to operate internationally, to profile what worked well and what did not.

At the same time, I was also doing research for my first book, The Internationalists: Business Strategies for Globalization.[3] *I decided to tour the world to interview expatriate executives. I could gather the specific scenarios of international experiences from the executives and professionals of major global corporations. My books addressed strategies relative to human capital.*

At first, she continued to work with the firm, but she resigned when it was clear that researching and writing the book required much more of her time and attention.

Being an Internationalist is a passion for Cathy, and by the year 2000, the role of an Internationalist had become a distinct profession.

Recognized academic institutions such as INSEAD in Fontainebleau, France, the American Graduate School of International Management (Thunderbird) in Phoenix, and Harvard's Program for Global Leadership offer creative, thoughtful programs for the international executive.[4]

In her books, Cathy identified elements that are essential for living outside your comfort zone: learning the local language and establishing trust through sensitive and respectful interactions in everyday living. But her primary predictor of success became a mindset that manages expectations:

making sure that they [participants] understand that there is a cycle of cultural adjustment, and it is far deeper than might be imagined.

START WHEN THEY'RE YOUNG

Besides projects in Ukraine and Russia, Cathy has done in-depth travel in Central America, Mexico, Europe, and Eastern Europe. She and her second husband loved to camp in the Colorado mountains. It was during those trips that they developed stories for children, using animal characters who traveled to other countries. Then they had a grandson who could hear the stories. Cathy's daughter told her that these stories were so good that they should be written down.

Fifteen years ago, Cathy and her husband developed a new company. They cowrote a series of children's books titled *The Adventures of Simon and Barklee*[5] that described, in vivid detail, the fun to be had as best friends Barklee, the dog, and Simon, an operatic canary, journey to many countries in the world. In the introduction to *Simon and Barklee in West Africa*,[6] Cathy writes,

they knew there is no better way to learn about the world and its people than to experience them.

Their travels always feature a citizen of that country who serves as a guide who could point out and explain many aspects that are typical of that country and its people. Cathy developed a curriculum for the books, and they established an educational platform. The books were used extensively in private schools around the country, but they are no longer in print.

Cathy and her husband wanted to energize the natural curiosity of children and to motivate them to want to know more about others who shared the world.

Our intention was to grow global citizens by bringing the world to children through stories.

As Cathy remarked in our interview, when you travel extensively and explore other cultures,

It's not possible to not be changed.

When she retired in 2010, she and her husband spent winters teaching

at a small little school in the middle of nowhere in Mexico. I raised money for them, and we built a library.

They continue to travel extensively.

EVER THE ACTIVIST

However, those were not her only endeavors in helping kids realize that they are part of the vast global community.

For two years, in Virginia, where they now live, she created a project she called Global Citizenship. Cathy enlisted an administrator at Old Dominion University and another at a small private school to help her to implement her program. Fifth-, sixth-, and seventh-grade students in the school had personal experiences and interactions with international college students to broaden their outlook.

It was very challenging, but I thought it was pretty cool. And I will arrange to have that continue [without me].

Once a month, Old Dominion sends a student to give a presentation about his or her home country. There have been graduate students, postdoctoral students, and researchers from all over the world.

The younger students gain person-to-person experience with a citizen from another land; the international students have the chance to interact with youngsters who may not have come into their circle naturally. One of the keys to the success of these experiences is Cathy's willingness to respond to the individual circumstances of each encounter. The common thread that she uses is attention to the particular visitor and the context of the visit. That meant no scripts or formulaic presentations. To paraphrase the philosopher Heraclitus, "you cannot step into the same river twice."[7]

Cathy has found a significant way to humanize a stranger, to put a face on another country, and to instill the beginning of an appreciation of its culture. Her far-reaching experience as a global citizen informs her point of view; when she sees opportunities to widen the exposure of others, she helps them to expand outside their circle of familiarity.

TRY THIS AT HOME

What would you encourage parents, teachers, and others who have kids in their lives today to do?

I would recommend, as early as possible, to bring kids together from many different cultures. Interestingly, young kids don't see the differences. They play together no matter what. It doesn't matter what color you are or what language you speak. They can somehow figure it out.

But expose teenagers to international life, preferably there in another country or here or in whatever way is possible. I know not everyone can afford to travel, but just learning about another culture can foster a sense of global citizenship, an understanding that we are not just citizens here where

we live. Everything is connected, everyone is connected, and we can under-
stand how those connections work.

Today, at seventy-seven, Cathy is deciding what the next leg of her journey will be, a journey to reveal the strong universal values and characteristics we all share, and fascinating and distinct differences we have to learn. Cathy believes that ultimately, this recognition will shine a bright light on our path to peace, the hope that lives in the hearts of all who consider ourselves international citizens.

HOW TO CONNECT!

"About AFS." American Field Service (AFS-USA), Intercultural Programs USA
  https://www.afsusa.org/about-afs/
Evans, Hugh. "What Does It Mean to Be a Citizen of the World?" TED Talk.
  https://www.ted.com/talks/hugh_evans_what_does_it_mean_to_be
    _a_citizen_of_the_world?language=en
Scherer, Catherine W. *The Internationalists: Business Strategies for Globalization*. Wilsonville, OR: BookPartners, 2000.
———. *The Internationalists: Masters of the Global Game*. New York: Business Expert Press, 2010.

Stefanie Seltzer

1938

To have been born a Jewish child in Lodz (Łódź), Poland in 1938 was to have your destiny foretold. The German army would occupy the city in September 1939; in February of 1940, they would establish the infamous Lodz ghetto; they sealed it off from the rest of the city in April. When the ghetto was liquidated in August 1944, the surviving residents were sent to Auschwitz-Birkenau.

If you visit the US Holocaust Memorial Museum in Washington, DC, you will see a special exhibit about Lodz, once home to one of the largest Jewish communities in the world. Much has been written about child survivors—of hiding, internment, escapes, and survival during World War II—as those who still can bear witness and teach us reach their eighties and nineties.

In the introduction to the book *The Last Witness: The Child Survivor of the Holocaust*,[1] psychoanalyst Judith Kestenberg points to the value of lessons we can learn about all children who survive the horrors of persecution and separation from parents when she writes:

> We have tried to present some of the complexities of understanding the interplay of genocidal persecution and the development of the child, keeping in mind the uniqueness of the experience of each of these "last witnesses." We hope that readers will be able to tolerate the anxiety, horror, and sadness that this subject invariably evokes. It is a necessary experience if we are to prepare ourselves better to understand the survivors of massive trauma.

CHILD SURVIVOR

Child survivors are defined by Robert Krell, MD, as those who were eighteen or younger at the end of the war in 1945.[2]

Stefanie Fishman, an only child, survived through her mother's resilience and resourcefulness, the kindness and courage of Polish gentiles and even German soldiers, and her own strength.

My mother had me smuggled out of the ghetto when I was just a baby. Where did you hide?

One day, when I was speaking to a group of youngsters, one asked me how many hiding places I had been in, so I actually sat down and wrote them all down, and I realized I had been in seven different hiding places. Toward the end of the war, during the war's uprising, my mother came to get me from my last hiding place. She had found a place for me. I guess she thought I would be able to walk, but I had been hiding under the dining room table, shielded by the tablecloth, for over three months. The woman who was hiding me had a brother who lived in the same room, and he was a Jew hunter for the Gestapo. So I had a chamber pot under the table, but I was afraid to use it. I couldn't walk.

Her father's fate was unknown to Stefanie until, years later in America, an older cousin, who had been studying at Cambridge University in England before the war, told her. Her father had been killed when he left the ghetto to meet a gentile pharmacist friend to obtain medicine for a relative who was too ill to escape.

Stefanie and her mother survived the postwar years in displaced persons camps in Vienna, with emigration to Palestine, Australia, or the United States delayed by her mother's heart condition and Stefanie's having contracted TB. Finally, in 1952, they came to New York City. Stefanie was thirteen years old and now much the stronger of the two. After several disastrous marriages, her mother died in her early fifties.

THE NEW WORLD

Living in America meant growing up and growing past the history that had shaped Stefanie. She lived in New York, in Boston, and in Michigan while she acquired the formal education that would equip her to be a social worker and counselor. She married, had two sons. She divorced, married again, and had a daughter with the husband who became devoted father to all three children. He supported and encouraged her work with adolescents with behavioral disorders and mental illnesses at the famed Devereux School outside of Philadelphia. When she left that work, and later found her life's calling, his support and encouragement lasted until his death in 2004.

1985: AWAKENING

I didn't know I was going to start an organization. I was living in Downingtown, Pennsylvania, near Philadelphia.

In August of 1985, Dr. Judith Kestenberg convened a meeting of people who had survived as children as part of a larger gathering of Holocaust survivors at the old convention center in Philadelphia. I didn't know anybody there. I don't know how many of us were in the room, but many were there from all over the United States and Canada. Someone from Los Angeles, who became my dear friend, came to this meeting, and she stood at the head of the table and she said, "They tell us that we cannot remember because we were only children." And she said, "But I remember how they took the children by their legs and flung their heads against the wall."

And at that point, the room just fell apart. We were the last meeting of the conference. They turned off the air conditioner. It was stinking hot. They flickered the lights. None of us left. Finally, I said, "We have to get together again."

Dr. Kestenberg said, "You can't get together by yourself, you've been through too much trauma." And I said, "But we are here now." And I took out a couple of pieces of paper and asked who wanted to give their names and their phone numbers. And I walked up to her and I said, "Really, I think we have so much to talk about." She relented finally, and she gave me the names of people in Boston, in Washington, Baltimore, New York, and Detroit, all places where she had spoken and groups were forming. No one responded, but a group was in Malvern (not far from where I lived). I got in touch with these people, and about three weeks later I had a picnic in a park near where I lived. Thirty-five people came. Dr. Kestenberg came, and Eva Fogelman.[3]

Among the group was a man from nearby Lancaster, Pennsylvania, who owned a hotel and suggested that people who wanted to get together over a weekend could do so there at a special rate. Stefanie organized the gathering of the eighteen people who responded—"The Lancaster Eighteen," as they dubbed themselves.

I shared a room with two other women, and we talked through the entire night. When all of us met again in the morning we decided to plan for a big gathering the following year. Of course, this was before cell phones and home computers. By word of mouth, the news spread. The next year, 174 people came to Lancaster from Canada and throughout the United States. We were now a family. We grew to over 300 and outgrew the hotel. We decided that after three years in Lancaster, we would move to other cities.

You had formed a nonprofit organization?

Yes. A lawyer I knew helped me incorporate us. Then I applied for the 5013C status myself.

Why a separate organization for child survivors? There were active Holocaust survivor groups already.

Whenever I would approach the survivors, they would look me up and down, literally, and say, "But you were too young, what could you possibly remember?" I felt like I was the only one experiencing that. I think that all of us child survivors were experiencing that. That's why we formed this organization, officially the World Federation of Jewish Child Survivors of the Holocaust, an all-inclusive name. The name includes all who survived as children, regardless of the circumstances of their survival—whether in camps, via Kindertransports,[4] in hiding, or by escaping to Shanghai, Russia, and Siberia.

TODAY

Today, Holocaust Child, or "The Federation," as it speaks of itself, attracts between 300 and 500 attendees from around the world at its annual meetings. Meetings have been held in cities across the United States and Canada, from West Palm Beach, Florida, to Vancouver, British Columbia and also in Amsterdam, Prague, Jerusalem, Warsaw, and even Berlin.

Their speakers' bureaus and telling of survivors' stories have provided valuable personal testimonies and professionally prepared educational programs and experiences for thousands of schools and classrooms, as well as videotaped interviews for national and international archives documenting the Holocaust.

Descendants of survivors have been included; the founders recognized that next generations, too, have been deeply affected by their families' histories. The reunions serve as

an opportunity to bring together our next generations to inspire and remind them about the importance of remembrance and of education about what can happen when hatred and intolerance take hold—and the Federation's determination to fight hatred and genocide—of all peoples.

Stefanie divides her time between her home in Bala Cynwyd, Pennsylvania and the California desert, with travel for Holocaust Child and her own family, who are scattered geographically but emotionally close. Her children (emergency room physicians and a teacher) and grandchildren are, as she says, "all on the same page." Caring activists for social justice and for Holocaust Child.

Today, the work of Holocaust Child, the illumination and focus it brings on the effects of trauma in childhood, rarely examined before the enormity of the Holocaust, has more to teach us than ever—about the children of today.

HOW TO CONNECT!

Holocaust Child
   https://holocaustchild.org
US Holocaust Memorial Museum
   https://www.ushmm.org/

· *22* ·

Ram Singal

FOR GOODNESS' SAKE

$\mathscr{I}$t is one of the coldest days of the winter. The wind slices through Manhattan's bitter atmosphere like hundreds of sharp needles headed for the same target. Ram Singal, tall, smiling broadly, and moving briskly, appears in the lobby of the building just as we take refuge from the outside. We ride the elevator to the Meditation Center and sit in welcoming warmth to talk about this organization's *7 Billion Acts of Goodness* and the life events that brought him to this commitment.

As a young man in Moga, in the Punjab state of India, Ram learned about Brahma Kumaris, a worldwide spiritual movement that supports the cultivation of a deep collective consciousness of peace and of the individual dignity of each soul.[1]

Founded in India in 1937, the widespread effects of this organization have reached 110 countries on all continents. He dedicated his life to their nonsectarian mission when he was twenty-one.

Ram finished his civil engineering degree in India and came to the United States to work as a professional engineer. He worked in the World Trade Center, where he helped to develop the structural integrity inspections for the north tower. Then he trained inspectors to perform those inspections.

IN THE HEART OF THE STORM

All of this became critically important on September 11, 2001, when Ram, then nearly fifty, found himself on the sixty-fourth floor of the north tower of the trade center when the plane hit. His firsthand knowledge proved to be invaluable as he struggled to guide other survivors down the building's staircases to the ground. But even in the urgency of those moments, he noticed that as he reached out to help people escape the crumbling tower, he did not experience fear. Later he realized that his paramount concern, to get the other victims out of the crippled building, had dominated his natural instincts. Fear could not coexist with the desperate need to help.

In the aftermath of the tragedy, for about ten days, Ram did not follow the newspaper and TV reports. Instead, he explains that he had a profoundly positive experience in the disaster by helping people, and he did not want to lose that. He said to himself,

Ram, do not look back, move forward. You cannot bring it back. There was a reason you survived the World Trade Center tragedy. Forgiveness.

He was surprised to find that he had done so much work in the World Trade Center that he felt an overwhelming emptiness in his heart. Many urged him to give interviews, to file health insurance claims, to find a way to seek revenge against the perpetrators of the attack.

REVENGE?

I told them, I got saved. Isn't that enough? In a time of crisis, you can always find someone else in more pain or more fearful than you are. Then your own fear disappears.

Forgiveness is not just refusing to take revenge. In that case, you send the person away empty-handed. Real forgiveness means not only do you resist revenge, but you send that person away feeling something good about himself. Then the person can say, "Ah! he made me feel light. It's not that I'm going away empty."

Yes, I have forgiven him, but he must forgive himself. So you show him some of his good qualities. Then you send him total forgiveness. You turn your

anger into forgiveness, your anger into compassion, your anger into love. Then we can say that peace works.

In the days following, as Ram rose from survivor's guilt, he began to ask himself, "Why was I saved? What do I want to do now?" His habit of daily meditation helped him to discover the answer: the rest of his life would be lived in the service of humanity. He reflected on the 9/11 events. He wondered how he could use those experiences for benefit and good. If one great act of evil could shake the world, could acts of goodness shake it too? Could a negative event be turned into a positive plan?

Three years later an idea took form when Ram saw an issue of *Time* magazine. The cover story claimed that happiness could be as "contagious" as the flu virus. There had been a twenty-year longitudinal study of 5,000 people.[2] It concluded that, unknowingly, people are drawn to a happy person. In fact, they could track four distinct levels of happy individuals who also become happy because of that influence. If that could happen, Ram reasoned, why couldn't acts of goodness have a similar effect? Why couldn't one good act shake the world? He noted that Einstein's theory of nuclear energy states that the chain reaction, once begun, cannot be stopped—in simple layman's terms, a domino effect.

Ram had observed that fear drives us in many ways. Why not have *goodness* drive us instead? But to make this an attractive and motivating concept, goodness would have to be dynamic, exciting.

He believes that goodness is part of the DNA of humanity. Looking back on his life experiences, Ram could list many times when people performed acts of goodness, actions that required going beyond what was expected, even beyond a person's perceived capacity. He realized that goodness could be defined as performing good acts even when it is inconvenient.

I have seen many, many times in my life when I went above and beyond my duty or obligation, it gave me such joy. When I did something by going out of the way I had such a good experience in my life.

For example, it's getting late, and you are in a rush. And somewhere you see an older man walking or needing help. You say, I want to help, but I'm late. Now if I am ready to take the trouble, let me help that person anyway. That is going out of your way.

Back home in India, if somebody has to give one hundred rupees to some-one as a gift, they don't give one hundred. They always give one hundred and one. Extra. Sometimes you give to me, sometimes I give to you. It's give and take. But one dollar, one rupee, one unit of kindness in the name of humanity that "extra" becomes part of the chain reaction.

At the same time, people often look for the grand act. It brings attention and respect on a large scale. But when there are small things to do, things others don't want to do, people can be turned off. They think small things will reduce their own value. But if we perform all acts with peace or happiness or love the effect is enhanced.

The thought came to mind: my value is not what I do, but whatever I do, I can put my value in that action and make that action valuable. So that is what an act of goodness is: grassroots people, ordinary people going out of their way for others with generosity. And doing what other people don't want to do.

We talk about changing the world or saving the world. To me, saving the world can only happen if you keep on rejuvenating it, one person at a time. And as an engineer, I want to know the process as well as the applica-tion, creating something.

But acts of goodness must be uncalculated. There is no give and take. By the act itself, I see the goodness coming back to the individual. It is based on achievement and enjoyment. The result inspires others. Meditation and yoga powers are not just for solutions. They are for uplifting the spirit.

These thoughts and experiences led Ram to create the program 7 *Billion Acts of Goodness.*[3] The name originates from the estimate at the time that the population of the world numbered seven billion. Ram believes that if we all collectively achieve that same number of acts of goodness, it can be "the tipping point needed for the explosion of good-ness and happiness" in the world—the chain reaction. He tested the pilot program with children and with a Christian group that declared it neutral (nondenominational). That is a quality that makes it appealing to so many more people.

I also know there are people out there who are looking for hope, looking for continuity, looking for the way to make a difference in the world. I cannot give up because I always see more potential.

To that end, Ram travels worldwide to show volunteer program leaders how it can be done and to help set the structure of the program. Trainees are then free to conduct the program. When a program is put in motion, Ram moves to another place to do the same again. No money changes hands. There is no charge for participation and no remuneration or profit for him or others in the program. Most of this project has been funded by Ram himself, through his own work and the simplicity of his lifestyle. Participants attend meetings and are helped to focus on rediscovering their own internal goodness. They fill out pledge forms and agree to spend one year performing their acts of goodness and reporting on the website. The tally is reflected in the counter on the program's website.

"IT IS NEVER TOO LATE."

Good work that transcends expectations, plus humility and love, results in spiritual energy. Spiritual energy—the energy of love, the energy of caring, the energy of enthusiasm—that is where I found goodness. Spiritual energy increases when we use it; it makes the acts of goodness perfect. And it is never too late.

HOW TO CONNECT!

Brahma Kumaris
  www.brahmakumaris.org/
Park, Alice. "The Happiness Effect." *TIME*, December 23, 2008.
7 Billion Acts of Goodness
  http://www.actsofgoodness.org/
  https://www.youtube.com/watch?v=6DnUs6i7MFA
7 Billion Acts of Goodness Blog
  http://www.actsofgoodness.org/blog/

· 23 ·

Rochelle Sobel

ASIRT, MAY 3 TO JULY 18, 1995

𝒯he Association for Safe International Road Travel was founded in July of 1995. Like many nonprofit organizations, ASIRT was born in the mind and heart of a grieving family member in response to tragedy. In the immediacy of shock and loss, Rochelle Sobel, until then, a high school English and Hebrew teacher, wife, and mother of four children, gathered her strength and that of the people around her in order to memorialize her third child. Aron had just been killed in a bus crash in Turkey two weeks before his graduation from the University of Maryland medical school.

Aron Sobel had finished his final rotation abroad at Hadassah Hospital in Israel and went to Turkey for a few days before coming home to graduate and start his residency, which would be in Boston. On May 3, along with twenty-two other passengers from many countries, he was on a bus speeding down the wrong lane of a narrow, ill-maintained road with a sharp curve and no guardrail—a road that had long been on a government list of "black spots" in need of repair. Everyone on the bus was killed. July 18 would have been his twenty-fifth birthday.

As a future physician, Aron's dream was to be able to save lives, so it seemed natural that we would save lives in his honor. It seemed logical.

On that day, July 18, ASIRT was officially born, a nonprofit organization dedicated to improving road safety for tourists and other travelers around the world.

THE MAKING OF AN ACTIVIST

The Sobel family had moved from Chicago, where Rochelle's husband was in private medical practice, to Maryland, in the suburban Washington, DC area. Dr. Solomon Sobel (deceased, February 2019) had been called to work at the FDA. Rochelle, prepared with degrees in English literature and education from the University of California, American University, and George Washington University, taught English and Hebrew at Jewish day schools. Their surviving son and daughters are, respectively, a psychiatrist, a medical doctor, and a clinical psychologist.

FIRST STEPS

We did it together, my family and, really, the community around us. The community were very supportive and creative. The first thing we did was have a vigil in front of the Turkish Embassy in Washington. We lit candles for all of the twenty-three people who were killed. We had tall candles with the names of each of the countries the people were from, Great Britain, Germany, the United States, and Turkey. Many Turkish people came down from the embassy and asked if this was part of a political, anti-Turkish movement. We explained exactly what it was, and they became very supportive. Some wanted to help and said they had lost cousins and uncles in accidents. One of the people who came subsequently joined our organization and was on the board. We became very friendly with several of the ambassadors who later served in that embassy.

At first, when Aron was killed in 1995, I really felt like a lone voice in the wilderness because road crashes were not recognized as a global health issue. I went to the State Department at that point and asked them how many people die abroad, and how many Americans die in road crashes. They said they didn't know. And I asked them what the roads are like in Turkey, and they said "we really don't know that much." And when I asked them how many people died in road crashes in general globally, they said they didn't know.

ANALYZING THE PROBLEM

The mandate of the International Travel division of the State Department is to protect American citizens traveling abroad, so we decided to become the organization that did know. And we started to learn.

Road crashes are the single greatest cause of death for young people ages five through twenty-nine globally, far exceeding deaths from AIDS, tuberculosis, and malaria. Close to 1.4 million people die every year on the roads, and an additional fifty million are injured; most are young people.

Clearly, the immediate problem was ignorance. Even our own State Department not only lacked information, but alarmingly, lacked awareness. Yet how many millions of young people like Aron, from countries all over the world, travel, work, and study abroad, eager to learn about each other, other cultures, and themselves? Did no one realize how many never may get home?

Not too many years later, the World Health Organization [WHO] called us and said they were forming an organization for road safety globally and asked if we could join them. We are a member of that organization and many others that have sprung up since then, so it has grown as a real movement.

DOING THE WORK

Starting a nonprofit organization is always challenging. Doing it through the trauma of loss had to be exceptionally so. But it was done. The seed money was about $5000, which came from the lawsuit against the bus company. Fund-raising and building an organization began immediately. The structure of ASIRT has worked effectively from the outset. The board, now about eight members, serve voluntarily. Also voluntary are about the same numbers of world-renowned experts from around the world. The executive director, an IT person, and a researcher are paid, as are occasional part-time staff as needed. Rochelle, who has led the group and been chief writer, editor, and spokesperson, has never been paid. World organizations support travel, as do companies who request their expertise. An early five-year grant was provided by Mayor Bloomberg of New York.

Our approach has always been nonconfrontational. It is always to work with whatever countries we are working with, whatever organizations we are working with, in the belief that working together forms the best energy and helps action take place and improvements occur.

Through the years, through embassies in Washington, we have been invited to come to many countries where they set up meetings for us with ministers of transport, ministers of health, and ministers of the interior. We come to them with our story and with the facts that they can do a lot to prevent road crashes. The whole concept behind our story is that these deaths are preventable. Through the WHO we have been working with a group of organizations called UN Road Safety Collaboration, and among us all we've had many road safety resolutions passed.

I have spoken at ministerial conferences, like one scheduled for 2020 in Sweden where we bring ministers together to work on what kinds of things can be done to reduce road crashes. We now have a worldwide organization, through our WHO group, that consists of NGOs from all over the world involved in this issue.

We have formed a caucus in Congress working toward global road safety and through them we have gotten resolutions passed for road safety. Every year someone from Congress and from the Senate stands up and addresses the issue, marks the third Sunday in November as World Remembrance Day for Road Crash Victims and their families, and puts it in the Congressional and Senate records to continuously raise awareness.

So we tackle it in a variety of ways. We are involved with corporations that send staff abroad, and with humanitarian and study abroad programs, so they have the knowledge of what risks they will find within the countries they send people to, and what's the best way to prevent those risks and plan itineraries to reduce risk. They can rely on road travel reports we prepare on about eighty countries throughout the world.

At our annual gala, several of which have been held in the Turkish Embassy here in Washington, we recognize and give awards to people who have made major contributions to road safety.

Perhaps the scope and effect of Rochelle's work can best be viewed from the perspective of ASIRT's inaugural summit, held on May 13, 2019 at the US Congressional Visitor Center, called Safe Travel and Tourism: Paving the Way, a Road Safety Travel Summit. It was led by Rochelle, by now a well-known figure in halls of government around the world.

The summit brought together representatives from the tourism and hospitality industries, US and other government agencies, the insurance industry, tourism ministries and embassies, and education abroad. Senator Chris Van Hollen was among the speakers. Rochelle pointed out that tourism accounts for one-tenth of the global GDP and is a key driver of economic growth. While people are traveling increasingly for many reasons, and at great benefit to themselves and their host countries, they are traveling increasingly to low- and mid-economic countries, where most road crashes occur. According to the Centers for Disease Control and Prevention, nearly one-half of the medical evacuations back to the United States are the result of a road crash. The forecast for the number of international tourists killed or seriously injured on the roads is not good.

TODAY

Rochelle's eightieth birthday, in November of 2020, is not likely to mark a slowing down of activity, let alone of commitment and dedication to the work she does for a cause that was revealed through tragedy. She continues as founder and president of ASIRT, and its chief spokesperson. Her life is very full, with activism, her children and grandchildren, and still, as needed, by teaching English and Hebrew to high school students.

HOW TO CONNECT!

Association for Safe International Road Travel
https://www.asirt.org/

IX

CONFESSION OF A
rEVOLUTIONARY

That's not a printing error. It describes a process. The process begins with awareness that something that really matters to you is wrong. The awareness leads to learning and acquiring accurate information about the wrong.

Information gathering reveals that you are not alone. In fact, a virtual revolution in public awareness and consciousness-raising is going on! Finding one of the like-minded groups focused on the same problem turns out to be very easy: speaking to friends and neighbors, noticing groups that have formed in my community, checking out the topic on Google—all yield the necessary info.

I enlist in the struggle to fight, reform, improve, fix, cure, oust _____ (fill in the blank.)

My activism is part of the revolution. I love being a rEvolutionary!

Eventually, I realize that what has happened for me is more than being part of the revolution. It has triggered my own evolution. While I have been doing my small part to fix a problem, I have been learning about myself, too.

I've learned that I have something, maybe a lot, to give that is outside of myself. I've felt the security and strength of community. I've learned new skills and revived some old ones. I've felt the strength that comes from confronting what is most wrong.

On the other hand, I've kept evolving and learning how to see the other side of any argument, to really listen, to know when my enthusiasm is falling on deaf ears, to see how compromise works, to "read" my audience of one or more, to keep my mind open for more growth and development. I'm evolving all the time.

I love being a rEvolutionary!

TR

Rosaline Tompkins

YOUNG ELDER

*W*hat does it take to be an Elder? Is it merely age, or is it dedication, the respect of others, and perceived wisdom? Rose, as Rosaline is called, was born in 1962, which does not suggest the term applies in the prevailing culture's sense. And yet, through her dedication to her own people and to humanity in general, she has been setting an example of kindness and activism for years—being, therefore, an Elder. A motivational speaker and a woman who struggles for survival on the one hand and on the other can build a kitchen and cook for older people protesting the oil pipeline at Standing Rock, and lead others as they retrace the Trail of Tears,[1] Rose is an inspirational figure far beyond her own tribe and beyond the Native American community. She is currently living in Columbia, Missouri.

I'm considered an Elder because I'm actually fighting for the Native American rights . . . standing up and protecting our earth, our community, looking out for the needs, whether they be health or personal or financial needs, for the elders and the younger generation on reservations.

SOME RECENT AMERICAN HISTORY

Rose was born in Hawthorne, California, far from her tribal home in Montana, at the Fort Peck Reservation, home to the Assiniboine and Sioux tribes. It lies sixty miles south of Canada and seventy miles west of the North Dakota state line. This was because of federal policy in the late 1950s and 1960s that took men from their reservations and moved them to cities where they could be trained in various skills. Rose's father was moved to California, where he became a licensed plumber so that he could return to the reservation and teach others to become plumbers.

When did you go to Montana?

At the age of four.

ROSE'S STORY

When I was about six years old, the Bureau of Indian Affairs (BIA) came to the families' homes, took the kids out of their homes, and put them in board-ing schools across the United States. So I went to a boarding school in North Dakota at the age of six, and I stayed there until I was nine.

I don't think I'll ever get over the sadness I felt. Being taken away from Grandmom, being taken away from Mom and Dad, being put in a boarding school with all these strangers. I got spanked for the very first time there. I had my hair pulled for the very first time. I had my mouth slapped. My hands were hit with a ruler. They forced us to go to these boarding schools so that they could colonize us into European ways. You know, sit up straight, don't talk back, speak English, all that stuff, so it was very hard. I think I was almost eight years old when I got paddled because I tried to run away. And my bottom was filled with blisters, water blisters, and one of my sisters snuck out and was able to call my dad in Montana and he flew over there.

Rose's father took his five children out of the boarding school, assuring them he would not let the government take them anywhere again. Unfortunately, he was powerless when the BIA soon struck again.

They came to all the homes and all the kids that were in the homes at the time were taken from their homes and put in Christian foster homes until the age of thirteen. All of us. There are so many people on my res-ervation right now that still remember their foster homes and what hap-pened there. It was horrible. This was the time in the 1960s and the early 1970s when the government was trying hard to get us to speak English, to be religious.

FAMILY INTERRUPTED

What has been the effect on your family?

When you're put in all different foster homes and come back when you are thirteen, you don't know your sisters and brothers anymore. We have all been taught differently, different religions, even if they are all Christian. The foster home was the first place I was molested. I tried telling my foster mom; she slapped me on my hand and told me not to be making up stories. It was horrible. And who are we and where are we supposed to go? We don't know anybody. We are in the white man's world, and these people are taking care of us. We have nobody that we can call. We have nobody that we can contact and tell them what is going on.

I feel so bad for my parents. My mom up and left my dad when we were put in the boarding schools. She went to North Dakota to the Standing Rock Reservation, her original home, and stayed there. My dad drove us all the way to North Dakota from Montana so we could spend time with her. She is ninety now and still hurts a lot. She doesn't know how to treat any of us kids because she was never there to be a mom. So now we hug her and kiss her and tell her, "We don't blame you, Mom." If I can get my own place here, it's only $186 to go home on the train and get my mom and bring her back to stay with me.

My dad took his own life in 1989. He had colon cancer and did not want to be a burden to any of us girls, who were all married and had our own families.

Rose married at eighteen. Her three children, two sons and a daughter, all college-educated and working, live on the reservation in Montana and care for their father, who has ALS.

A SPIRITUAL AWAKENING AND PRACTICE

Religion has no place in my life. It's all about spirituality. I believe there is one creator, the one that gives us spirituality and our morals and values.

Is there a moment or event that stands out in your spiritual journey?

In actuality, I started back in the early 1980s. A girlfriend and I used to go to Sun Dance in Green Grass, South Dakota. Chief Arvol Looking Horse is there; he is the Keeper of the White Buffalo Calf Pipe, and he invited us to meet. We became protectors of the earth from that time on. I was twenty-three.

I follow the traditions and practices of sun-dancing, attending sweats [sweat lodge ceremonies], and smudging, using natural herbs and medicines to help take care of myself as well as others.

What is "smudging"?

We use four sacred things: sage, cedar, sweetgrass, and tobacco, to cleanse ourselves, to have blessings, to have ceremonies. I have a little rock bowl, and I crumble up some sage into a ball, light it on fire, and then I put a little bit of cedar on it and it snaps and crackles and smells so good! We take the smoke and we swish it on our hair and face. We do this to our head first because that's where we must stay focused—within our mind, in our head.

And then we blow the smoke at our heart because that purifies our heart. That purifies our spirit and helps us to stay good all day long. Like not to judge, lie, steal, or cheat.

And then a lot of times we take that smoke and we rub it underneath our feet. We do that because we don't know where our footsteps are going to take us that day, but we want each footstep to count as a prayer. That will help us as a guide to stay on the right path.

ROSE'S PATH

While Rose worked hard at many jobs, she was determined to further her education. In 2014 she went to college, a path that was interrupted when in 2016

the dogs came to attack the protestors or the protectors of the land at the Dakota Pipeline in Standing Rock and I couldn't take it anymore. I just loaded all my stuff up, put it in storage, and I have been on the road ever since.

ROSE'S KITCHEN AT STANDING ROCK

Much has been written about the protests in Standing Rock that resulted in the Obama administration's denial of a key permit for the Dakota Access Pipeline (the denial since rescinded by the Trump administration). In the service of others, Rose did something she had never done before. Here is her story:

In August of 2016, I went to Standing Rock to be a Prayer Warrior. As a diabetic, I must eat a good breakfast; then I have a light lunch and finish supper around 7:00. One night after supper I walked up to the sacred fire, and there were so many elderly people sitting around there, all waiting to be fed, which wouldn't happen until 9:30 or 10:00. I heard a few of them complaining about it, so the next day I decided to cook and [give them] whatever I had left over. I had my friends help carry my pots and some paper bowls up there to all the elders to feed them.

I started doing that every evening around 6:30 or 7:00. One day I just got on the microphone and invited all elders to my camp and told them where it was and that I would feed them every day so they could be in bed by 9:00.

In October, some people in the camp came to me and said they knew what I was doing and offered to give me my own kitchen, which they would supply with groceries. When they asked what I wanted to call it, I said, "Rose's Kitchen." I started cooking every day on an open fire, and at the end of October a woman came from Wisconsin and said, "If you could have a kitchen, what kind would you want?" I said a big one, like an army camp one. Not even six days later, a big truck pulled into the camp, and I'll be darned if they didn't unload a huge army tent. Within a half-hour, there were twenty to thirty guys outside ready to put that tent up for me.

Rose's Kitchen lasted until February of 2017. She left just ten days before the camps were raided by dozens of National Guard and law enforcement officers in a military-style takeover, one day after a deadline for the camp's eviction. Since then she has been invited to speak in many places. While she continues to work to sustain herself, her dedication to her beliefs and to her people and her family drive all her actions. Recently, Rose wrote to me,

The Trans-Canadian Keystone pipeline is trying to push their way through our dam . . . FORT PECK DAM . . . our water source along with thousands of others'. My tribal people on the reservation are gearing up for the protection of all of our lands and water, attending meetings for protest and how to prevent physical harm with prayer. My heart cries and I want to see our Mother Earth receive all the respect back that has been taken from her. She is breaking to pieces below our feet; an inferno is rising through storms of hurricanes, tornados, fires, floods, and volcanoes. I hope I can continue to do what I can to help, to participate, to help others to rise up and stand in solidarity.

Rose hopes someday to live among her children and hoped-for grandchildren on her home reservation in Montana.

HOW TO CONNECT!

Help Native Americans
    https://www.powwows.com/category/blog/
Keep Up with Climate Change and Activism
    https://insideclimatenews.org/
Native American Culture
    https://www.warpath2peacepipes.com/native-american-indians/
Volunteer on an Indian Reservation
    https://globalvolunteers.org/usa-montana/

Notes

CHAPTER 1: MIGNON S. ADAMS

1. See https://www.sociologyguide.com/thinkers/Tonnies.php.

2. Gabi Redford, "New Technologies Help Seniors Age in Place—and Not Feel Alone," *USA Today*, March 11, 2018, https://www.usatoday.com/story/money/2018/03/11/new-technologies-help-seniors-age-place-and-not-feel-alone/389897002/.

3. Ina Jaffe, *Meet a Home Contractor Who Helps Older People Age in Place*, NPR, May 31, 2017, https://www.npr.org/2017/05/31/528949740/meet-a-home-contractor-who-helps-older-people-age-in-place.

4. Ilyce Glink, *10 Smart Home Features to Help You Age in Place*, CBS News, October 10, 2017, https://www.cbsnews.com/media/10-smart-home-features-to-help-you-age-in-place/.

5. Judith Graham, "Want to Stay Strong as You Age? Find a Purpose," *Washington Post*, September 24, 2017, https://www.washingtonpost.com/national/health-science/want-to-stay-strong-as-you-age-find-a-purpose/2017/09/22/afcc6152-9d7b-11e7-8ea1-ed975285475e_story.html.

6. SeniorAdvisor.com blog, "Senior Cohousing: A Trend in Senior Living," May 13, 2019; "Cruise Ship Retirement 101," February 20, 2016; "15 Senior Living Trends," last updated May 6, 2019.

7. GW Public Health Online blog, "The Rise of Aging-in-Place Villages," April 12, 2016, https://publichealthonline.gwu.edu/blog/rise-of-aging-in-place-villages/.

8. Chris Bentley, "Why More Seniors Are Forming Their Own 'Villages,'" Citylab.com, September 17, 2015, https://www.citylab.com/life/2015/09/why-seniors-are-forming-villages-to-age-in-place/405583/.

9. See https://www.vtvnetwork.org/content.aspx?page_id=22&club_id=691012&module_id=238482&actr=4.

10. Erin Arvedlund, "Get-together." *Philadelphia Inquirer*, Philly Edition, January 15, 2017, http://www.friendscentercity.org/sites/default/files/attached_fiels/Inquirer%201_15_17%20Erin%20Arvedlund%20article.pdf.

CHAPTER 5: BETH DOLAN

1. See https://archive.org/stream/AnAchievableVisionReportOfThe DepartmentOfDefenseTaskForceOnMental/MHTF-Report-Final_djvu.txt p ES-4.

2. See https://www.antioch.edu/seattle/resources/community-resources/ institute-war-stress-injuries-recovery-social-justice.

3. Jon Krakauer, *Where Men Win Glory: The Odyssey of Pat Tillman* (London: Atlantic, 2010).

4. Amir Bar-Lev, Mark Monroe, and Joe Bini, *The Tillman Story*, directed by Amir Bar-Lev; produced by John Battsek.

5. See http://strangerathome.org/. Author's note: Military.com began in 1999 to revolutionize the way the thirty million Americans with military affinity stay connected and informed. Today, it is the largest online military and veteran (free) membership organization.

6. Patricia Kime, "Active-Duty Military Suicides at Record Highs in 2018," Military.com, January 30, 2019, https://www.military.com/daily-news/ 2019/01/30/active-duty-military-suicides-near-record-highs-2018.html.

7. Kime, "Active-Duty Military Suicides."

8. Kime, "Active-Duty Military Suicides."

9. Meghann Myers, "Suicides among active-duty soldiers are up about 20 percent," ArmyTimes.com, https://www.armytimes.com/news/your-army/2019/ 02/04/suicides-among-active-duty-soldiers-are-up-about-20-percent/.

10. See https://eeginfo.com/.

11. See http://homecoming4veterans.org/.

CHAPTER 6: PEGGY ELLERTSEN

1. "Faces Behind the Screen: Peggy." 3Play Media, January 16, 2018, https:// www.3playmedia.com/resources/faces-behind-screen/peggy/.

2. American Speech-Language-Hearing Association, *Aural Rehabilitation for Adults*, https://www.asha.org/Practice-Portal/Professional-Issues/Aural -Rehabilitation-for-Adults/.

3. "Faces Behind the Screen: Peggy."

CHAPTER 9: KENDALL HALE

1. Heinz Stucki, "After the Bombing," *OnWisconsin* (Fall 2010): 63, https://onwisconsin.uwalumni.com/campus-news/after-the-bombing/.

2. Author's note: On July 30, 1942, President Franklin Roosevelt signed the Navy Women's Reserve Act into law, creating what was commonly known as the WAVES—Women Accepted for Volunteer Emergency Service—a division of the US Navy created during World War II to free up male personnel for sea duty. See https://dod.defense.gov/News/Article/Article/1102371/remembering-navy-waves-during-womens-history-month/.

3. Robin Morgan, ed., *Sisterhood Is Powerful: An Anthology of Writings from the Women's Liberation Movement* (New York: Vintage, 1970).

4. Kendall Hale, *Radical Passions: A Memoir of Revolution and Healing* (Bloomington, IN: iUniverse, 2008).

5. See https://www.ncwarn.org/our-work/atlantic-coast-pipeline/; https://www.bloomberg.com/news/articles/2019-03-25/duke-needs-plan-b-if-atlantic-coast-pipeline-fails-ceo-says-jtot9ovj.

6. Hale, *Radical Passions*.

PART IV: SOCIAL MEDIA AND THE NEW SENIOR MOMENT

1. Kirk Kristofferson, Katherine White, and John Peloza, "The Nature of Slacktivism: How the Social Observability of an Initial Act of Token Support Impacts Subsequent Prosocial Action," *Journal of Consumer Research* 40, no. 6 (2014): 1149–66.

CHAPTER 10: LYNN HOLBEIN

1. See https://en.wikipedia.org/wiki/List_of_rallies_and_protest_marches_in_Washington,_D.C.#1950%E2%80%931999.

2. Stephen Solomon, "The Controversy over Infant Formula," *New York Times Magazine*, December 6, 1981, 92, https://www.nytimes.com/1981/12/06/magazine/the-controversy-over-infant-formula.html.

3. Solomon, "Controversy over Infant Formula."

4. Philip J. Hilts, "6 1/2 -Year Boycott of Nestle is Ended as Firm Adopts Baby Formula Code," *Washington Post*, January 27, 1984, https://www.washingtonpost

.com/archive/politics/1984/01/27/6-12-year-boycott-of-nestle-is-ended-as-firm
-adopts-baby-formula-code/24552e48-7920-449a-a5fd-0baa1f13ab66/?utm
_term=.4bc98f44f1c0.

5. History.com, https://www.history.com/this-day-in-history/reagan-refers
-to-u-s-s-r-as-evil-empire-again.

6. See https://www.helencaldicott.com/about/.

7. See http://lindastout.org/about.

8. Richard Halloran, "House, 245-176, Votes Down $988 Million for
MX Missile; Setback for Reagan Policy," *New York Times*, December 8,
1982, https://www.nytimes.com/1982/12/08/us/house-245-176-votes-down
-988-million-for-mx-missile-setback-for-reagan-policy.html.

9. Linda Stout, *Bridging the Class Divide: And Other Lessons for Grassroots
Organizing* (Boston: Beacon, 1996).

10. See https://spiritinaction.net/about-us/who-we-are/linda-stout/.

11. Concord Prison Outreach (CPO), https://www.concordprisonoutreach
.org/.

12. See http://partakers.org/college-behind-bars/.

13. UU Mass Action, https://www.uumassaction.org/awards.

14. Susan Cheever, "The Secret History of the Serenity Prayer," *The Fix*,
March 6, 2012, https://www.thefix.com/content/serenity-prayers-desperate
-origins-Niehbur-Bonhoeffer-Tillich9965.

CHAPTER 11: LYNNE ISER

1. Lisa Katz, "Tzedakah: More Than Charity," https://www.thoughtco
.com/tzedakah-more-than-charity-2076098.

2. ALEPH, "Rabbi Zalman Schachter-Shalomi," https://aleph.org/reb
-zalman.

3. Sage-ing International, https://www.sage-ing.org/.

4. Lynne Iser, "Becoming an Elder-Activist: My Kitchen Table Transformation," https://www.sage-ing.org/becoming-elder-activist-kitchen-table
-transformation/.

5. Sage-ing International, https://www.sage-ing.org/.

6. Pachamama Alliance, https://www.pachamama.org/about.

7. Pachamama Alliance, "Mission & Vision," https://www.pachamama
.org/about/mission.

8. Joanna Macy & Her Work, https://www.joannamacy.net/main.

9. "Welcome," Joanna Macy & Her Work, https://www.joannamacy.net/
main#books.

10. "Welcome," Joanna Macy & Her Work.

11. Joanna Macy and Chris Johnstone, *Active Hope: How to Face the Mess We're in Without Going Crazy* (Novato, CA: New World Library, 2012). Out of print; replaced by Joanna Macy and Molly Young Brown, *Coming Back to Life: The Updated Guide to The Work That Reconnects* (Gabriola Island, BC: New Society, 2014).

12. Elder Activists, "About Lynne Iser, Activist, Facilitator, Teacher," http://www.elder-activists.org/about-lynne.html.

13. New Jim Crow Group/#Blacklivesmatter, https://mishkan.org/new-jim-crow-studyaction-group.

14. Iser, "Becoming an Elder-Activist."

CHAPTER 12: DANA KELLEY

1. The site of the Roosevelt Warm Springs Institute for Rehabilitation and Roosevelt's Little White House State Historic Site.

2. Derald Wing Sue, *Race Talk and the Conspiracy of Silence: Understanding and Facilitating Difficult Dialogues on Race* (New York: Wiley, 2015).

CHAPTER 14: JEAN LYTHCOTT

1. Julie Lythcott-Haims, *How to Raise an Adult* (New York: St. Martin's, 2015); Julie Lythcott-Haims, *Real American: A Memoir* (New York: Holt, 2017).

PART VI: PSSST! LOOK OVER HERE . . .

1. Jane McGonigal, *SuperBetter: A Revolutionary Approach to Getting Stronger, Happier, Braver and More Resilient* (New York: Penguin, 2015).

CHAPTER 16: IRENE BARNES MEHNERT

1. Robert E. Alberti and Michael L. Emmons, *Your Perfect Right: Assertiveness and Equality in Your Life and Relationships*, 10th ed. (Oakland, CA: Impact, 2017).

2. Don Miguel Ruiz, *The Four Agreements: A Practical Guide to Personal Wisdom* (San Rafael, CA: Amber-Allen, 1997).

CHAPTER 19: PATRICIA ST. ONGE

1. Howard Thurman (1899–1981) was an African American philosopher, theologian, educator, and inspiration and/or mentor to civil rights leaders including Dr. Martin Luther King Jr. A noted scholar, he wrote twenty books, was the first African American to meet with Gandhi, and co-led the Church for the Fellowship of All Peoples in San Francisco with a white minister, Dr. Alfred Fisk.

PART VIII: BUBBLE, BUBBLE, TOIL AND TROUBLE . . .

1. J. Holt-Lunstad, T. B. Smith, M. Baker, T. Harris, and D. Stephenson, "Loneliness and Isolation as Risk Factors for Mortality: A Meta-Analytic Review," *Perspectives on Psychological Science* 10 (2015): 227–37.

CHAPTER 20: CATHERINE SCHERER

1. J. R. R. Tolkien, "The Riddle of Strider," Tolkien Gateway, http://tolkien gateway.net/wiki/The_Riddle_of_Strider.
2. Catherine W. Scherer, *The Internationalists: Business Strategies for Globalization* (Wilsonville, OR: BookPartners, 2000), 78–79.
3. Scherer, *The Internationalists*.
4. Scherer, *The Internationalists*, 140–41.
5. Catherine W. Scherer and David J. Scherer, "The Adventures of Simon and Barklee," http://www.simonandbarklee.com/.
6. Catherine W. Scherer, *Simon and Barklee in West Africa* (Langley, WA: ExplorerMedia, 2007).
7. Attributed to Heraclitus, a Greek philosopher of Ephesus (near modern Kuşadası, Turkey) who was active around 500 BCE.

CHAPTER 21: STEFANIE SELTZER

1. Judith S. Kestenberg and Ira Brenner, *The Last Witness: The Child Survivor of the Holocaust* (Washington, DC: American Psychiatric Press, 1996).
2. Robert Krell, *Child Holocaust Survivors—Memories and Reflection* (Victoria, BC: Trafford Publishing, 2007).

3. Eva Fogelman, *Conscience and Courage: Rescuers of Jews During the Holocaust* (New York: Anchor, 1994).

4. Holocaust Encyclopedia, (Kindertransport, 1938–40), https://encyclopedia.ushmm.org/content/en/article/kindertransport-1938-40.

CHAPTER 22: RAM SINGAL

1. See www.brahmakumaris.org/.

2. Alice Park, "The Happiness Effect," *Time*, December 22, 2008, 40–42.

3. 7 Billion Acts of Goodness, www.actsofgoodness.org/; see https://www.youtube.com/watch?v=6DnUs6i7MFA.

CHAPTER 24: ROSALINE TOMPKINS

1. See https://www.peoplesworld.org/article/trail-of-tears-walk-commemorates-native-americans-forced-removal/.

Discussion Guide

$\mathcal{I}$n the Introduction, the authors said, "This is a time when the lengthening of life coincides with an explosion of change." Do you still want to keep up with the changes taking place around you? What are some changes that are important to you, things that you find meaningful? Which changes do you see that you can't resolve in your mind?

When you look around in today's world, is there something meaningful to you that you think needs to be "fixed"? What have you learned through your life experience that could be a significant insight into a solution for this "fix"?

Each person in this book is using something they have inside themselves to make the human condition better. Does it occur to you that you have something to give that you hadn't realized you have? What is it?

Where are you in your life? Have the constraints of earning a living, raising children, preparing for the future eased at all? What would you choose to respond to if you had no limits?

Today there are many calls for help: some we sense when we look into another's eyes; some we witness face to face. Some we know because we recognize that things are not as they should be. What do you care about profoundly? Where could you use your skills and your passion to answer the call for help?

Between the chapters, there are essays on some of the aspects of aging. There is a running theme among them: to engage, act, contribute, grow. Is there a way to make room in your schedule, in your life, to embrace a passion? Can you see yourself using that theme, following those steps?

Curiosity can be a path to discovery. But discovery usually implies leaving the comfortable and familiar life that we settle into in our senior years. In chapters 15 and 20, Cirel and Cathy have built lives of discovery in very different ways. They also seem to be strongly motivated and decidedly fulfilled. Have you been curious about issues in your observations of life today? Can you apply your experience to engage in the dialogue these issues create? How?

There is no shortage of research about the positive effects of engagement, particularly in aging individuals. If you look at the word you see how it *includes* aging: eng*aging*. Would you enjoy more opportunities to broaden your perspective, to add to your connections? How would activism further that goal?

The people profiled in this book have chosen positive activism at a time when there is plenty of negative influence in the world. Do you think there is negative activism? If so, what could be done about it; what should be done about it?

Index

About the Authors

Thelma Reese, EdD, retired professor of English and of Education, created the advisory council for Hooked on Phonics and was its spokesperson in the 1990s. In that role, and as director of the Mayor's Commission on Literacy for the city of Philadelphia, she appeared frequently on television and hosted a cable show in Philadelphia. She was a founder of Philadelphia Young Playwrights, chaired the board of Children's Literacy Initiative, and organized the World Symposium on Family Literacy at UNESCO in Paris in 1994. She is a member of the national organization Life Planning Network and of her local positive aging group. She is co-author, with Barbara Fleisher, of *The New Senior Woman: Reinventing the Years Beyond Mid-Life* and *The New Senior Man: Exploring New Horizons, New Opportunities*, both published by Rowman & Littlefield, and has been an invited speaker at senior centers, senior living communities, and community centers about both books. A mother and grandmother, she lives in Philadelphia with her husband, Harvey Reese, author and artist.

BJ Kittredge, MEd, is a retired consultant to the healthcare industry. Her professional career began in the public school classroom where she taught elementary, middle, and high school. She was selected for the New Jersey Department of Education Academy for the Advancement of Teaching and Management. She served as chair of a district-wide K–12 science curriculum development project and was a Geraldine R. Dodge fellow at Wesleyan University.

She moved from the academic sphere into operations in a major Philadelphia accounting firm and then a small publishing company. From there she was the first director of training and development in the member services division of US Healthcare. There she worked on the design and implementation of the department transition to self-directed teams. She authored and delivered original management training, Speakeasy communication skills programs, operations manuals for new IT systems, and a system for performance evaluation. She is the widow of Patrick W. Kittredge, Esq., and a proud mother and grandmother.